MOEDIM

THE APPOINTED TIMES
FOR MESSIANIC BELIEVERS

MOEDIM

THE APPOINTED TIMES
FOR MESSIANIC BELIEVERS

J.K. McKee

messianicapologetics.net

MOEDIM
THE APPOINTED TIMES FOR MESSIANIC BELIEVERS

Cover photos: Istockphoto

Published by Messianic Apologetics, a division of Outreach Israel Ministries
P.O. Box 850845
Richardson, Texas 75085
(407) 933-2002

www.outreachisrael.net
www.messianicapologetics.net

Unless otherwise noted, Scripture quotations are from the *New American Standard, Updated Edition* (NASU), © 1995, The Lockman Foundation.

Unless otherwise noted, quotations from the Apocrypha are from the *Revised Standard Version* (RSV), © 1952, Division of Education of the National Council of the Churches of Christ in the United States of America.

Abbreviation Chart and Special Terms

The following is a chart of abbreviations for reference works and special terms that are used in publications by Outreach Israel Ministries and Messianic Apologetics. Please familiarize yourself with them as the text may reference a Bible version, i.e., RSV for the Revised Standard Version, or a source such as *TWOT* for the *Theological Wordbook of the Old Testament*, solely by its abbreviation. Detailed listings of these sources are provided in the Bibliography.

Special terms that may be used have been provided in this chart:

ABD: *Anchor Bible Dictionary*

AMG: *Complete Word Study Dictionary: Old Testament, New Testament*

ANE: Ancient Near East(ern)

Apostolic Scriptures/Writings: the New Testament

Ara: Aramaic

ATS: ArtScroll Tanach (1996)

b. Babylonian Talmud (*Talmud Bavli*)

B.C.E.: Before Common Era or B.C.

BDAG: *A Greek-English Lexicon of the New Testament and Other Early Christian Literature* (Bauer, Danker, Arndt, Gingrich)

BDB: *Brown-Driver-Briggs Hebrew and English Lexicon*

BECNT: *Baker Exegetical Commentary on the New Testament*

BKCNT: *Bible Knowledge Commentary: New Testament*

C.E.: Common Era or A.D.

CEV: Contemporary English Version (1995)

CGEDNT: *Concise Greek-English Dictionary of New Testament Words* (Barclay M. Newman)

CHALOT: *Concise Hebrew and Aramaic Lexicon of the Old Testament*

CJB: Complete Jewish Bible (1998)

DRA: Douay-Rheims American Edition

DSS: Dead Sea Scrolls

ECB: *Eerdmans Commentary on the Bible*

EDB: *Eerdmans Dictionary of the Bible*

eisegesis: "reading meaning into," or interjecting a preconceived or foreign meaning into a Biblical text

EJ: *Encylopaedia Judaica*

ESV: English Standard Version (2001)

exegesis: "drawing meaning out of," or the process of trying to understand what a Biblical text means on its own

EXP: *Expositor's Bible Commentary*

Ger: German

GNT: Greek New Testament

Grk: Greek

halachah: lit. "the way to walk," how the Torah is lived out in an individual's life or faith community

HALOT: *Hebrew & Aramaic Lexicon of the Old Testament* (Koehler and Baumgartner)

HCSB: Holman Christian Standard Bible (2004)

Heb: Hebrew

HNV: Hebrew Names Version of the World English Bible

ICC: *International Critical Commentary*

IDB: *Interpreter's Dictionary of the Bible*

IDBSup: *Interpreter's Dictionary of the Bible Supplement*

ISBE: *International Standard Bible Encyclopedia*

IVPBBC: *IVP Bible Background Commentary (Old & New Testament)*

Jastrow: *Dictionary of the Targumim, Talmud Bavli, Talmud Yerushalmi, and Midrashic Literature* (Marcus Jastrow)

JBK: New Jerusalem Bible-Koren (2000)

JETS: *Journal of the Evangelical Theological Society*

KJV: King James Version

Lattimore: The New Testament by Richmond Lattimore (1996)

LITV: *Literal Translation of the Holy Bible* by Jay P. Green (1986)

LS: *A Greek-English Lexicon* (Liddell & Scott)

LXE: *Septuagint with Apocrypha* by Sir L.C.L. Brenton (1851)

LXX: Septuagint

m. Mishnah

MT: Masoretic Text

NASB: New American Standard Bible (1977)

NASU: New American Standard Update (1995)

NBCR: *New Bible Commentary: Revised*

NEB: New English Bible (1970)

Nelson: *Nelson's Expository Dictionary of Old Testament Words*

NETS: New English Translation of the Septuagint (2007)

NIB: *New Interpreter's Bible*

NIGTC: *New International Greek Testament Commentary*

NICNT: *New International Commentary on the New Testament*

NIDB: *New International Dictionary of the Bible*

NIV: New International Version (1984)

NJB: New Jerusalem Bible-Catholic (1985)

NJPS: Tanakh, A New Translation of the Holy Scriptures (1999)

NKJV: New King James Version (1982)

NRSV: New Revised Standard Version (1989)

NLT: New Living Translation (1996)

NT: New Testament

orthopraxy: lit. "the right action," how the Bible or one's theology is lived out in the world

OT: Old Testament

PreachC: *The Preacher's Commentary*

REB: Revised English Bible (1989)

RSV: Revised Standard Version (1952)

t. Tosefta

Tanach (Tanakh): the Old Testament

Thayer: *Thayer's Greek-English Lexicon of the New Testament*

TDNT: *Theological Dictionary of the New Testament*

TEV: Today's English Version (1976)

TLV: Tree of Life Messianic Family Bible—New Covenant (2011)

TNIV: Today's New International Version (2005)

TNTC: *Tyndale New Testament Commentaries*

TWOT: *Theological Wordbook of the Old Testament*

UBSHNT: United Bible Societies' 1991 Hebrew New Testament revised edition

v(s). verse(s)

Vine: *Vine's Complete Expository Dictionary of Old and New Testament Words*

Vul: Latin Vulgate

WBC: *Word Biblical Commentary*

Yid: Yiddish

YLT: Young's Literal Translation (1862/1898)

What Are the Lord's Appointed Times?

One of the first areas of Torah observance which comes into play, when outside people enter into the Messianic movement and commit themselves to a Messianic lifestyle, is that of **the holidays.** The appointed times guide the yearly cycle of events which help to form Messianic identity.[1] The appointed times guide the yearly cycle of events that help to form Messianic identity. Messianic Believers do not observe mainstream Christian holidays such as Christmas or Easter, but rather remember the Biblically-prescribed holidays of God's Torah, which are first fully detailed in Leviticus 23. This can, unfortunately, be an area of high contention between Christians and Messianics (because of misunderstandings on both sides), but when emphasized properly, celebrating the God-ordained appointed times of Scripture can be a great blessing—a blessing that many have unfortunately missed out on. It can be a unique way of testifying to others of God's ongoing plan of salvation history—the past and future redemptive acts involving Yeshua the Messiah.

Many Christians today are aware of the Messianic movement, but they are not really aware of what it stands for, or various Messianic views relating to the Scriptures. Some Christians today, however, are fascinated by it, and such fascination often abounds in the area of the Biblical holidays.

A holiday, as we call it in English, is defined by *The American Heritage Dictionary* as, "A day on which custom or the law dictates a halt to ordinary business to commemorate or celebrate a particular event."[2] Another definition provided is very simply, "A holy day." American holidays may include the Fourth of July or Independence Day, Memorial Day, Veteran's Day, Flag Day, or Pearl Harbor Day. Each

---

[1] This article is reproduced from the author's book *Torah In the Balance, Volume I* (Kissimmee, FL: TNN Press, 2003/2009).

[2] William Morris, ed., *The American Heritage Dictionary of the English Language* (New York: American Heritage Publishing, 1969), 628.

one of these days memorializes a particular event or group of people in American society. If you are not an American, you still no doubt have various national holidays which define the important history and events of your culture. **The same is true if we are citizens of God's Kingdom.**

As Believers in Messiah Yeshua, we are all a part of the Commonwealth of Israel (Ephesians 2:11-12) or the Israel of God (Galatians 6:16). This does not just mean we are a part of Israel in some generic, detached way. Be we Jewish or non-Jewish, we are citizens of God's Kingdom of Israel. Our King has prescribed specific times when we are to come to Him, when we remember events in the history of Ancient Israel, which in turn picture His plan of salvation and redemption through Messiah Yeshua. It is the heritage that we are called to take hold of in a very real and significant way throughout the seasons of the year.

In this article, we will briefly review what the Lord's appointed times are, and their importance for us today.[3]

What does "appointed times" actually mean?

In the opening verses of Leviticus 23, it is directed, "The LORD spoke again to Moses, saying, 'Speak to the sons of Israel and say to them, "The LORD's appointed times which you shall proclaim as holy convocations—My appointed times are these"'" (vs. 1-2).

The Hebrew term for appointed time or "appointed festival" (ATS) is *moed* (מוֹעֵד), and its plural form is *moedim* (מוֹעֲדִים). It has a variety of meanings, including "appointed time, appointed place," and "*set feast* or *appointed season*" (BDB).[4] It "is also the worshiping assembly of God's people" and "may possibly be an early designation for the synagogue" (TWOT).[5] A *moed* is to be a special time between God's people and Him. The *ArtScroll Chumash* remarks that "*Moadim* are the days which stand out from the other days of the year. They summon us from our everyday life to halt and to dedicate all our spiritual activities to them....The *Moadim* interrupt the ordinary activities of our life and give us the spirit, power, and consecration for the future by revivifying those ideals upon which our whole life is based, or they eradicate such

---

[3] It should be emphasized that although this chapter uses Leviticus 23 as an outline, it would be inappropriate for any teacher or reader not to recognize that throughout the Torah, and indeed the Bible, additional instructions regarding these festivals are given. Leviticus 23 happens to be the most comprehensive Biblical chapter where all of the *moedim* are listed.

[4] Francis Brown, S.R. Driver, and Charles A. Briggs, *Hebrew and English Lexicon of the Old Testament* (Oxford: Clarendon Press, 1979), 417.

[5] Jack P. Lewis, "mô'ēd," in R. Laird Harris, Gleason L. Archer, Jr., and Bruce K. Waltke, eds., *Theological Wordbook of the Old Testament* (Chicago: Moody Press, 1980), 1:389.

evil consequences of past activity as are deadly to body and spirit and thus restore us to lost purity and the hope of blessing."[6]

The "Tent of Meeting," where Moses and Aaron and the elders of Israel met the Lord in the wilderness, is called the *ohel moed* (אֹהֶל מוֹעֵד), which could be understood as the "tent of appointment." Numbers 20:6 details, "Then Moses and Aaron came in from the presence of the assembly to the doorway of the tent of meeting and fell on their faces. Then the glory of the LORD appeared to them." Using this as a frame of reference, if we truly want the glory of God to appear before any us, then the importance of meeting Him when *He wants*—not just whenever we want to meet Him—should be realized. Relegating the appointed times to past history, or ignoring them completely, is not something that is wise for students of the Scriptures.

The Hebrew term used for "convocation" in Leviticus 23:1-2 is *miqra* (מִקְרָא), and it specifically means, "**convocation**," "**assembly**," and a "**reading (aloud)**" (*CHALOT*).[7] It is derived from the verb *qara* (קָרָא), one possible meaning of which is "**recite from, read aloud** from (book, scroll)" (*CHALOT*).[8] The appointed times do call God's people together for them to remember what He has done for us in His Word, and recalls us to the heritage that we have going all the way back to the beginning. Consulting relevant passages of the Bible, and the important lessons that they teach us, is something surely witnessed when the appointed times are honored.[9]

Many Messianic Believers, especially those who place a high prophetic emphasis on the pattern of the Biblical appointments, define them as *rehearsals*. Certainly, when we celebrate the Biblical holidays we not only remember the historical events in the life of Ancient Israel such as the Passover and Exodus or the giving of the Ten Commandments, but we also recognize the prophetic fulfillment—both past *and* future—of Messiah Yeshua in them. We essentially "rehearse" what is to come, in preparation for the Messiah's return.

The Apostle Paul noted how the Biblical appointments "are a shadow of the things to come, but the substance belongs to Christ" (Colossians 2:17, ESV). The outline which the appointed times give us, is to naturally point to the Messiah. The Greek word for "substance" here is *sōma* (σῶμα), and while it is translated as "body" in some Bibles (KJV, NKJV, LITV), "substance" is by far better. It is better because

---

[6] Nosson Scherman, ed., et. al., *The ArtScroll Chumash, Stone Edition*, 5th ed. (Brooklyn: Mesorah Publications, 2000), 682.

[7] William L. Holladay, ed., *A Concise Hebrew and Aramaic Lexicon of the Old Testament* (Leiden, the Netherlands: E.J. Brill, 1988), 212.

[8] Ibid., 323.

[9] "This word can also mean reading in the sense of a public reading or that which is read in such a meeting" (Warren Baker and Eugene Carpenter, eds., *Complete Word Study Dictionary: Old Testament* [Chattanooga: AMG Publishers, 2003], 662).

the true meaning of the *moedim* is found in Messiah Yeshua. The Biblical festivals paint a pattern of His First Coming and sacrifice for our sins at Golgotha (Calvary), *and* they portray how He will return at His Second Coming, gather the saints, defeat His enemies, and establish His Kingdom. And, we would point out that this prophetic pattern of the holidays is not just something believed by Messianics, either. It is notable that many evangelical Christians express an interest in the Biblical festivals for this very reason, and recognize the important gospel lessons that they contain.

For those of us who celebrate these holidays, why do we do it? Certainly, the reasons are varied. **Obeying and wanting to please the Lord at the times that He wants us to should top the list.** We should "meet" Him when He wants to be met. He has specified throughout the Torah when He wants to be met and specific days that He wants to see consecrated unto Himself. If we meet Him on these days and follow the instructions, He should reveal His presence to us in a very profound and special way. But if we do not, and we believe in arrogance that we can meet at replacement times that are solely of our own choosing, what will happen? Will He still show up? Or, will those choosing not to celebrate His appointed times be left alone? While we can surely meet with God even now in prayer, the appointed times are important moments when we are to focus on Him in very specific ways.

The author of Hebrews admonishes, "let us consider how to stimulate one another to love and good deeds, not forsaking our own assembling together, as is the habit of some, but encouraging *one another*, and all the more as you see the day drawing near" (Hebrews 10:24-25). What is this "assembling together" spoken of? The Greek *episunagōgē* (ἐπισυναγωγή) just means "*a gathering* or *being gathered together*" (*LS*).[10] AMG adds, "Thus it would have the meaning of not betraying one's attachment to Jesus Christ and other believers, not avoiding one's own personal responsibility as part of the body of Christ."[11]

When we understand this in light of the Biblical holidays representing the pattern of Yeshua's First and Second Comings, as many think that the season of His return is probably approaching—we should not forsake the festivals of the Lord given to us in the Torah. We should realize that we are responsible to observe them, because they depict His redemptive plan for humanity, and most importantly the salvation message of Yeshua. Corporately, we should come together at each of the appointed times, and press into God in a very distinct way, desiring

---

[10] H.G. Liddell and R. Scott, *An Intermediate Greek-English Lexicon* (Oxford: Clarendon Press, 1994), 303.

[11] Spiros Zodhiates, ed., *Complete Word Study Dictionary: New Testament* (Chattanooga: AMG Publishers, 1993), 640.

Him to reveal Himself to us! These are to be times when we find ourselves bonded together in significant unity as the Body of Messiah.

Shabbat: The First Appointed Time

The first appointed time that the Lord prescribes is the Sabbath or *Shabbat* (שַׁבָּת), opening the list seen in Leviticus 23: "For six days work may be done, but on the seventh day there is a sabbath of complete rest, a holy convocation. You shall not do any work; it is a sabbath to the LORD in all your dwellings" (Leviticus 23:3). It is the day of the week that God has made a holy convocation—a time for us to be in special fellowship with Him.

The precedent for *Shabbat* is established all the way back in Genesis 2:3: "Then God blessed the seventh day and sanctified it, because in it He rested from all His work which God had created and made." The Sabbath is a weekly reminder of who God is and a proclamation that He is indeed Creator and in control of the Earth. Because *Shabbat* is designated as being on the *seventh day*, it is a reminder to us as Believers, many of whom have been taught in the past that the Sabbath was either done away with or changed (discussed further), that the Lord indeed is the only One in control of Creation.

Every week in Jewish homes prayers are offered to the Lord on *Shabbat* that recognize He created the world, and rested after His six creative acts were complete. They proclaim that He is the Creator God and that He controls the universe. Consider the implications if all of us repeated that God gave people the Sabbath, as a special gift to rest, every week. We would recognize that the Sabbath is to be kept because *there is indeed a God* and we are His people. We would recognize our Creator's Lordship, and His control of the universe.

The Sabbath is the time when God rested from His work, and so it is to be for us as well. It is to be a time of physical abstention from labor and a separated convocation for us to spend time with Him. While the Jewish tradition contains much we can benefit from in observing *Shabbat*, the need to rest in Him should have even more significance for us as Believers in Yeshua. We are told in Hebrews 4:9, "There remains therefore a Sabbath rest for the people of God." But this Sabbath rest cannot be some generic rest where in our minds we claim to rest, but our bodies are still working. We must take a complete rest and spend the day focused on our Heavenly Father, our Messiah Yeshua, and the Scriptures. The rest that we experience on *Shabbat* gives us a foretaste of what eternity is to be like.

Paul wrote in 1 Thessalonians 5:23, "Now may the God of peace Himself sanctify you entirely; and may your spirit and soul and body be preserved complete, without blame at the coming of our Lord Yeshua the Messiah." While these are multiple parts of our being, they still have to function together. God has commanded that we have a complete rest of our entire beings each week, not one of just our minds or spirits—but also of our bodies. In our hectic world today, taking a physical *Shabbat* rest is something that every Believer can benefit from! There are many testimonies from today's Messianic Believers (non-Jewish *or* Jewish) who missed out on the blessings of *Shabbat* rest in the past, but are now keeping the Sabbath. Many of you know the joy that *Shabbat* is, taking a complete day off and dedicating it entirely to the Lord and to fellow Believers.

This is something that many have sadly not had. Yet as many are diligently seeking God and asking Him to convict them of areas of their lives which need to be changed, many are being convicted about the importance of *Shabbat*. Furthermore, it is also important that many are realizing how *Shabbat* is one of the *moedim* or appointed times. It is notable that while many Christian Bible teachers have written on the Biblical holidays, and have helped to stir a great deal of interest in this subject matter, they commonly gloss over the Sabbath. Is this perhaps because they do not want Christians to consider *Shabbat*? If they were to write on the Sabbath as one of the appointed times, after all, is it possible some Christians will start asking questions and may even start to keep it? These people might wonder why Sunday Church really is not a "sabbath." How important is it for today's Believers to recapture a theology of "rest"?[12]

Passover/*Pesach*

The second of the Biblical *moedim* that God prescribes is *Pesach* (פֶּסַח), or Passover. It is specified, "In the first month, on the fourteenth day of the month at twilight is the LORD's Passover" (Leviticus 23:5). Of all the Biblical holidays, this is probably the one with which most Christians are familiar. Their familiarity with Passover is no doubt due to the fact that the Exodus of the Ancient Israelites from Egypt **is one of the most important themes in the Bible**,[13] as it depicts the Holy One of Israel as the God of freedom, able to deliver people from slavery, but also as it depicts our Exodus as born again Believers from death in sin to new life in Yeshua. The Angel of Death would *pass*-over the homes of the Egyptians, and if the blood of the lamb were not over the doorposts, the firstborn would die. Using this typology in relation to our faith in the Messiah, if we do not have His blood covering us, then we will suffer the second death—eternal damnation.

Observance of *Pesach* in ancient times is specified in the Torah. Here were just some of the requirements:

---

[12] For resources on how to keep *Shabbat* with your family, consult the *Messianic Sabbath Helper* by Messianic Apologetics.

[13] Consult the author's article "The Message of Exodus."

1. Families were to sacrifice a blameless lamb for their household: "each man is to take a lamb for his family, one for each household" (Exodus 12:3, NIV).

2. The blood of the lamb was to be placed on the doorposts and lintel of the house: "Moreover, they shall take some of the blood and put it on the two doorposts and on the lintel of the houses in which they eat it" (Exodus 12:7).

3. When eating of the Passover lamb, families were to eat it with unleavened bread and bitter herbs: "They shall eat the flesh that *same* night, roasted with fire, and they shall eat it with unleavened bread and bitter herbs" (Exodus 12:8).

4. Passover was to be observed for all of the generations of the Israelites: "It is a night to be observed for the LORD for having brought them out from the land of Egypt; this night is for the LORD, to be observed by all the sons of Israel throughout their generations" (Exodus 12:42).

Exodus 12:26-27 issues an important instruction: "when your children say to you, 'What does this rite mean to you?' you shall say, 'It is a Passover sacrifice to the LORD who passed over the houses of the sons of Israel in Egypt when He smote the Egyptians, but spared our homes.' And the people bowed low and worshiped." Knowing the scenes of the original Passover are to cause God's people to approach Him with great awe and reverence.

Passover was originally to be celebrated and remembered as a time when God showed His mighty power to the Egyptians and delivered His people into freedom. It is, in essence, Israel's first national holiday. It is to be a special time when we are to honor our Heavenly Father for the deliverance of the Ancient Israelites from their slavery in Egypt, and how He spared the firstborn by the shed blood of the lambs. It is something that we are to instill in offspring so that they might remember the power of God. J.H. Hertz describes this in more detail:

"The children of successive generations are to be instructed at Passover as to the origin and significance of the Festival. In the Seder service on the first two nights of Passover, this command has found its solemn realization. In it we have history raised to religion. The youngest child present asks the Questions, which are answered by a recital of the events that culminated in the original institution of Passover. Education in the home is thus as old as the Hebrew people."[14]

We must all admire the tenacity of the Jewish people for instilling this, as particularly witnessed in the Passover traditions of the *haggadah*

---

[14] J.H. Hertz, ed., *Pentateuch & Haftorahs* (London: Soncino, 1960), 257.

(הַגָּדָה), the traditional order of service used for one's *Pesach* meal at home and/or with one's congregational community.[15] Hopefully, as many of today's non-Jewish Believers come to the realization that they too can take a hold of Passover, they will see the need of similarly instilling Scripture as *all of our history* to future generations—because as Messianic Believers in Yeshua, Passover has a greater significance and importance than just the Exodus from Ancient Egypt.

The events surrounding Passover are significant to all people of faith. The Apostle Paul wrote the Corinthians, "For I do not want you to be unaware, brethren, that our fathers were all under the cloud and all passed through the sea" (1 Corinthians 10:1). Every person who partakes of salvation in Israel's Messiah benefits from the Exodus—and even more!

Pesach has a great significance as it relates to the sacrifice of the Messiah for the forgiveness of our sins. Yeshua is the blameless Lamb of God. John the Immerser proclaimed, "Behold, the Lamb of God who takes away the sin of the world!" (John 1:29), and the Apostle Peter wrote that the redeemed are covered "with precious blood, as of a lamb unblemished and spotless, *the blood* of Messiah" (1 Peter 1:19). Most important, Paul says in 1 Corinthians 5:7, "For our *Pesach* lamb, the Messiah, has been sacrificed" (CJB). Yeshua's sacrifice for us is to be understood as a blameless Passover lamb, killed so that we can have His blood covering the doorframe of our hearts.

Yeshua's Last Supper meal was in actuality a Passover *seder*. This is recognized by many Christians today who are beginning to celebrate and remember Passover in their churches, as a useful educational tool for reconnecting with the Old Testament. This is often how many evangelical Believers (including my own family) get exposed to the Messianic movement.

For people of faith, Yeshua's Last Supper is often one of the most important scenes in Scripture, depicting the agony that our Lord endured prior to His execution (Matthew 26:39). The importance of Passover is seen in how the Messiah told His Disciples, "I have earnestly desired to eat this Passover with you before I suffer" (Luke 22:15).[16]

The Last Supper is summarized for us in Matthew 26:18-19; 26-28:

"And He said, 'Go into the city to a certain man, and say to him, "The Teacher says, 'My time is near; I *am to* keep the Passover at your

---

[15] Consult Joseph Tabory, *JPS Commentary on the Haggadah* (Philadelphia: Jewish Publication Society, 2008), for an overview of the traditional Passover *haggadah*, as well as its historical development and use in the Synagogue.

[16] From this Last Supper is derived the common Christian practice of communion with the bread and the wine—although in its proper context the Lord's Supper should be practiced with *matzah* or unleavened bread, not leavened bread, and probably only once a year during the *seder* meal. Consult the FAQ on the Messianic Apologetics website "Communion."

house with My disciples.""" The disciples did as Yeshua had directed them; and they prepared the Passover...While they were eating, Yeshua took *some* bread, and after a blessing, He broke *it* and gave *it* to the disciples, and said, 'Take, eat; this is My body.' And when He had taken a cup and given thanks, He gave *it* to them, saying, 'Drink from it, all of you; for this is My blood of the covenant, which is poured out for many for forgiveness of sins.'"

Commemorating Passover today should be a great time of remembrance and celebration for us as Messianic Believers, as well as a time of reverent severity. We remember the Exodus from Egypt, and we remember the Last Supper and sacrifice of Yeshua on the cross for the remission of our sins. We remember the original Passover in Egypt, and compare it to what happened at Golgotha (Calvary). We see a great correlation of the Ancient Israelites being brought forth from bondage into freedom, and born again Believers being brought out of sin into forgiveness.

In addition to remembering *Pesach* for the events of the past, we also remember it for the future. Yeshua told His Disciples, "'for I say to you, I shall never again eat it until it is fulfilled in the kingdom of God.' And when He had taken a cup *and* given thanks, He said, 'Take this and share it among yourselves; for I say to you, I will not drink of the fruit of the vine from now on until the kingdom of God comes'" (Luke 22:16-18). We still recognize that there is a future Passover coming, when the cycle will be complete, as the Messiah will be ruling and reigning from Jerusalem.

The Festival of Unleavened Bread/*Chag HaMatzah*

Concurrent with the remembrance of Passover—and in Jewish tradition witnessed in the New Testament and today often just called by the general season "Passover"—is the Festival of Unleavened Bread:

"Then on the fifteenth day of the same month there is the Feast of Unleavened Bread to the LORD; for seven days you shall eat unleavened bread. On the first day you shall have a holy convocation; you shall not do any laborious work. But for seven days you shall present an offering by fire to the LORD. On the seventh day is a holy convocation; you shall not do any laborious work" (Leviticus 23:6-8).

The Festival of Unleavened Bread is called *Chag HaMatzah* (הַמַצָּה חַג) in Hebrew. It was instituted so that the Ancient Israelites would remember eating the bread of haste that they had to prepare quickly as they left Egypt. There was no time to let their bread rise, so instead they were forced to eat it unleavened. Unleavened bread or *matzah* (מַצָּה) was required to be eaten on the first night of Passover, and then was to be eaten for the week following:

"Now this day will be a memorial to you, and you shall celebrate it *as* a feast to the LORD; throughout your generations you are to celebrate it *as* a permanent ordinance. Seven days you shall eat unleavened bread, but on the first day you shall remove leaven from your houses; for whoever eats anything leavened from the first day until the seventh day, that person shall be cut off from Israel" (Exodus 12:14-15).

Deuteronomy 16:3 notes how the Ancient Israelites were to eat Unleavened Bread so that they would remember their affliction in Egypt: "You shall not eat leavened bread with it; seven days you shall eat with it unleavened bread, the bread of affliction (for you came out of the land of Egypt in haste), so that you may remember all the days of your life the day when you came out of the land of Egypt."

The Festival of Unleavened Bread is observed by removing all leavened items from one's house. You are probably aware of the many "Kosher for Passover" items available during this time, as leavening items such as yeast have been removed from many products for use during the Passover season.

As Believers in Messiah Yeshua, the Festival of Unleavened Bread takes on very important meaning for us. Hertz validly states that "Leaven is the symbol of corruption, passion and sin,"[17] which is *exactly* what Yeshua took upon Himself when He was crucified. The Messiah spoke of leaven in Matthew 16:6 when He said, "Watch out and beware of the leaven of the Pharisees and Sadducees," in reference to some of their teachings which were non-Scriptural and were no doubt sinful.

The Apostle Paul emphasizes in 1 Corinthians 5:8, in relation to Passover, "Therefore let us celebrate the feast, not with old leaven, nor with the leaven of malice and wickedness, but with the unleavened bread of sincerity and truth," encouraging Believers that when they celebrate this holiday, they are to get the leaven or sin out of their lives. During the Passover season we participate in *Chag HaMatzah* by eating unleavened bread for seven days. Each time we pick up a piece of *matzah*, we should be consciously reminded of Yeshua's sacrifice for us, as He is the sinless, leaven-less, Bread of Life. Interestingly enough, Yeshua was born in Bethlehem or *Beit-Lechem* (בֵּית-לֶחֶם), a name which means "House of Bread."

As Messianic Believers commemorate the week of *Chag HaMatazah* or the Feast of Unleavened Bread, we must be reminded of the prophecy of Isaiah 53:5: "But he *was* wounded for our transgressions, he *was* bruised for our iniquities: the chastisement of our peace *was* upon him; and with his stripes [Heb. sing. *chaburah*, חַבּוּרָה] we are healed" (KJV). Many Messianics have validly compared this prophecy to the beatings of Yeshua, who was scourged and mocked and shamed

---

[17] Hertz, 256.

for us (cf. Matthew 27:26-31; Mark 15:15-20). Those of you who have seen *matzah* know that it has "stripes" and small holes in it, and it is indeed "flat," or leavenless. When we partake of *matzah*, it should hopefully remind us of the true Bread of Life, who is Messiah Yeshua. He was leavenless and without sin as the Bread of Life, and was the atonement for us by His sacrifice. He indeed had to take the punishment due us, incurred by our sin, onto Himself (Colossians 2:14).

We observe the Feast of Unleavened Bread today as a reminder of the Ancient Israelites' trek from Egypt and the bread of haste that they had to eat. But we also observe it in remembrance of Messiah Yeshua, who came as the leaven-less, or sinless Lamb of God, beaten and bruised for us. Every· time we see *matzah*, we are to be reminded of what He endured for us.

The Waving of the Sheaf

An important ceremony, known as the waving of the sheaf of first fruits, was to be observed in conjunction with the Festival of Unleavened Bread:[18]

"Then the LORD spoke to Moses, saying, 'Speak to the sons of Israel and say to them, "When you enter the land which I am going to give to you and reap its harvest, then you shall bring in the sheaf of the first fruits of your harvest to the priest. He shall wave the sheaf before the LORD for you to be accepted; on the day after the sabbath the priest shall wave it"'" (Leviticus 23:9-11).

This first fruits offering was commanded to be presented before God, during the season of Passover and Unleavened Bread. Because there is no Temple any longer in which the priest can wave the *omer* (עֹמֶר) or sheaf of first fruits, or present the proper offerings, its celebration was largely discontinued in Judaism after the Romans destroyed Jerusalem.[19] Leviticus 23:11-14 describes the kinds of offerings God expects to have presented to Him at this time:

"He shall wave the sheaf before the LORD for you to be accepted; on the day after the sabbath the priest shall wave it. Now on the day when you wave the sheaf, you shall offer a male lamb one year old without defect for a burnt offering to the LORD. Its grain offering shall then be two-tenths *of an ephah* of fine flour mixed with oil, an offering by fire to the LORD *for* a soothing aroma, with its drink offering, a fourth of a hin of wine. Until this same day, until you have brought in the offering of your God, you shall eat neither bread nor roasted grain

---

[18] Please note that as important as the waving of the sheaf ceremony is for understanding prophetic typology, that the Torah does not specify it as "*Chag HaBikkurim*" or the "Festival of First Fruits," as is common in some Messianic circles.

[19] Consult the entry for "firstfruits" in Jacob Neusner and William Scott Green, eds. *Dictionary of Judaism in the Biblical Period* (Peabody, MA: Hendrickson, 2002), 228.

nor new growth. It is to be a perpetual statute throughout your generations in all your dwelling places."

Yeshua the Messiah fulfilled the typology of firstfruits via His resurrection. Paul asserts in 1 Corinthians 15:17, "if Messiah has not been raised, your faith is worthless; you are still in your sins." This was the time when the high priest or *ha'kohen ha'gadol* (הַכֹּהֵן הַגָּדוֹל) would enter into the Temple and wave the first fruits of the harvest before the Lord. It is representative of Yeshua's being raised for us, as He is the first fruits of those who have been raised from the dead:

"But the fact is that the Messiah *has* been raised from the dead, the firstfruits of those who have died" (1 Corinthians 15:20, CJB).

Yeshua's resurrection from the dead as first fruits—assures us that there will be a future resurrection of all redeemed saints into the restored Kingdom of God on Earth (1 Corinthians 15:12-14)![20]

Pentecost/*Shavuot*

Beginning during the season of Passover and Unleavened Bread is a counting of weeks to the Festival of Weeks:

"You shall also count for yourselves from the day after the sabbath, from the day when you brought in the sheaf of the wave offering; there shall be seven complete Sabbaths [seven full weeks, RSV, NIV, CJB, ESV, et. al.]. You shall count fifty days to the day after the seventh sabbath; then you shall present a new grain offering to the LORD...On this same day you shall make a proclamation as well; you are to have a holy convocation. You shall do no laborious work. It is to be a perpetual statute in all your dwelling places throughout your generations" (Leviticus 23:15-16, 21).

Shavuot (שָׁבֻעוֹת) is known to many by its Greek-derived name Pentecost or *Pentēkostē* (πεντηκοστή), meaning "fiftieth." Its Hebrew name is derived, however, from the plural form of *shavua* (שָׁבוּעַ), which means "week," in reference to the seven weeks which are to be counted to *Shavuot*. In Exodus 34:22, *Shavuot* is described as being "the Feast of Weeks, *that is*, the first fruits of the wheat harvest, and the Feast of Ingathering at the turn of the year." Deuteronomy 16:9-10a further specifies how God's people are to "count seven weeks for yourself; you shall begin to count seven weeks from the time you begin to put the sickle to the standing grain. Then you shall celebrate the Feast of Weeks to the LORD your God with a tribute of a freewill offering of your hand" (Deuteronomy 16:9-10a).[21]

---

[20] For a discussion on what transpires in the intermediate time between death and resurrection, consult the author's article "To Be Absent From the Body."

[21] Note that the command to count "from the day after the sabbath" (Leviticus 23:15) has been interpreted differently for at least 2,300 years. During the time of Yeshua, the Sadducees considered "the sabbath" here to be a reference to the weekly *Shabbat*, whereas

Shavuot was originally intended to be an agricultural festival, where primarily the first of the wheat harvest would be presented to the Lord as a special offering, in the form of bread, waved before Him:

"You shall bring in from your dwelling places two *loaves* of bread for a wave offering, made of two-tenths *of an ephah*; they shall be of a fine flour, baked with leaven as first fruits to the LORD. Along with the bread you shall present seven one year old male lambs without defect, and a bull of the herd and two rams; they are to be a burnt offering to the LORD, with their grain offering and their drink offerings, an offering by fire of a soothing aroma to the LORD. You shall also offer one male goat for a sin offering and two male lambs one year old for a sacrifice of peace offerings. The priest shall then wave them with the bread of the first fruits for a wave offering with two lambs before the LORD; they are to be holy to the LORD for the priest" (Leviticus 23:17-20).

Since the destruction of the Temple, additional importance has been applied to *Shavuot*. Hertz indicates, "Jewish tradition…connects it with the Covenant on Mount Sinai, and speaks of the festival as…'the Season of the Giving of our Torah'. The Israelites arrived at Sinai on the New Moon. On the second of the month, Moses ascended the mountain; on the third, he received the people's reply; on the fourth, he made the second ascent and was commanded to institute three days of preparation, at the conclusion of which the Revelation took place. Hence its association with the Feast of Weeks, which became the Festival of Revelation."[22] H.M. Adler further comments, "With the destruction of the Second Temple, the agricultural aspect of the Festival receded, and Shavous became primarily the Feast of Revelation."[23]

Shavuot, referred to here as the Feast of Revelation, is readily associated with God giving Moses the Ten Commandments on Mount Sinai, which is certainly something worthy of celebration and convocation. The giving of the Ten Commandments, and indeed the entire Torah, is something that is monumental for all of humanity—arguably second to the resurrection of Messiah Yeshua! Without the Torah, we would be unable to see the Messiah to whom it points (Romans 10:4, Grk.)!

However, in realizing the traditional connection between *Shavuot* and the giving of the Law, we see that the first *Shavuot* was not as glorious as one might make it out to be. While Moses was on the mountain receiving the commandments from God in an awesome scene of fire and smoke, the Ancient Israelites were forsaking God and

---

the Pharisees interpreted it as a reference to the High Sabbath of Unleavened Bread. In Judaism today, the Pharisaical method is what is followed. Messianic practice invariably differs.

Consult the FAQ on the Messianic Apologetics website "*Omer* Count."

[22] Hertz, 521.

[23] Cited in Ibid.

making themselves a golden calf. We know the story all too well from Exodus 32, as when Moses came down from the mountain, he smashed the tablets:

"It came about, as soon as Moses came near the camp, that he saw the calf and *the* dancing; and Moses' anger burned, and he threw the tablets from his hands and shattered them at the foot of the mountain. He took the calf which they had made and burned *it* with fire, and ground it to powder, and scattered it over the surface of the water and made the sons of Israel drink *it*" (Exodus 32:19-20).

A cry of war went out in the Israelite camp because of this grave and terrible sin. Moses called those loyal to God to his side and ordered that they slay those who were sinning:

"Now when Moses saw that the people were out of control—for Aaron had let them get out of control to be a derision among their enemies—then Moses stood in the gate of the camp, and said, 'Whoever is for the LORD, *come* to me!' And all the sons of Levi gathered together to him. He said to them, 'Thus says the LORD, the God of Israel, "Every man *of you* put his sword upon his thigh, and go back and forth from gate to gate in the camp, and kill every man his brother, and every man his friend, and every man his neighbor."' So the sons of Levi did as Moses instructed, and about three thousand men of the people fell that day" (Exodus 32:25-28).

Three thousand Israelites were killed in association with this first *Shavuot* because they sinned against the Lord and worshipped an idol. However, thirteen hundred years later in Jerusalem, as *Shavuot* was required to be one of the three pilgrimage festivals (Deuteronomy 16:16), this appointed time experienced some important prophetic fulfillment. At this time, just after Yeshua had ascended into Heaven, the Apostle Peter proclaimed a riveting message to those assembled in Jerusalem:

"Men of Israel, listen to these words: Yeshua the Nazarene, a man attested to you by God with miracles and wonders and signs which God performed through Him in your midst, just as you yourselves know—this *Man*, delivered over by the predetermined plan and foreknowledge of God, you nailed to a cross by the hands of godless men and put *Him* to death…Therefore let all the house of Israel know for certain that God has made Him both Lord and Messiah—this Yeshua whom you crucified" (Acts 2:22-23; 36).

Acts 2:41 states that "there were added about three thousand souls." On the first *Shavuot*, or the day of Pentecost as it is widely known, three thousand died because of their idolatry. Thirteen hundred years later, on the day of Pentecost, three thousand came to faith in the Messiah.

The Book of Acts describes how on this *Shavuot*, people believing in the Holy One of Israel from all over the known world came to gather in Jerusalem, both those who were observant Jews and proselytes (Acts 2:9-11). Contrary to popular belief, Peter did not proclaim to the crowds amassed the beginning of "the Church." Rather, he proclaimed the good news and that Yeshua was both "Lord and Messiah" (Acts 2:36). What Peter proclaimed was that He is the promised Redeemer of Israel, and that those assembled were to "Turn from sin, return to God, and each of you be immersed on the authority of Yeshua the Messiah into forgiveness of your sins, and you will receive the gift of the *Ruach HaKodesh*! For the promise is for you, for your children, and for those far away—as many as *ADONAI* our God may call!" (Acts 2:38-39, CJB).[24]

The events at this *Shavuot* are extremely important for us to remember today. It was the time when the Holy Spirit came to dwell in all the Believers, as the close and personal presence of God: "And suddenly there came from heaven a noise like a violent rushing wind, and it filled the whole house where they were sitting. And there appeared to them tongues as of fire distributing themselves, and they rested on each one of them. And they were all filled with the Holy Spirit and began to speak with other tongues, as the Spirit was giving them utterance" (Acts 2:2-4). Prior to this time, the Holy Spirit was only given to kings of Israel, prophets, and those specifically anointed by the Lord—but now, all who had faith in Yeshua were given the Spirit! This new work of God, inaugurated at *Shavuot*/Pentecost, was preparing to change the world.

When we celebrate *Shavuot* now, there is much to be thankful for and to remember. We first remember the baked loaves and offerings that were to be presented to the Lord as a pleasurable aroma to Him. We then remember what we should consider to be the second most important event in our faith (the first being the Messiah's resurrection): the giving of the Ten Commandments to Moses at Mount Sinai. And as Messianic Believers, we are reminded that on the *Shavuot* following the Messiah's ascension into Heaven that the Holy Spirit was poured out and that many were saved, decisively beginning the era of the New Covenant (cf. Acts 15:8-9).[25]

---

[24] For a further discussion, consult the author's article "When Did 'the Church' Begin?"

[25] For resources on how to keep the Spring festivals with your family, including the Festival of *Purim* (Esther 9:26-27), consult the *Messianic Spring Holiday Helper* by Messianic Apologetics.

The Day of Blowing/*Yom Teruah*
Rosh HaShanah

The Summer season does not include any Biblically-mandated times of appointment, and so the cycle of *moedim* does not pick up again until the Fall or Autumn:

"Again the LORD spoke to Moses, saying, 'Speak to the sons of Israel, saying, "In the seventh month on the first of the month you shall have a rest, a reminder by blowing *of trumpets*, a holy convocation. You shall not do any laborious work, but you shall present an offering by fire to the LORD""" (Leviticus 23:23-25).

The first of the Fall *moedim* is known as *Yom Teruah* (יוֹם תְּרוּעָה) or the Day of Blowing, also commonly called the Feast of Trumpets. *Teruah* (תְּרוּעָה) means "shout or blast of war, alarm, or joy" (*BDB*).[26] All of these definitions play out on *Yom Teruah*, as God's people are commanded to have a holy convocation and enjoin themselves to one another. It is to be a day of rest so that we might be properly called into a time of extreme holiness. In Judaism today, *Yom Teruah* is called *Rosh HaShanah* (רֹאשׁ הַשָּׁנָה) and is celebrated as the Civil New Year. In Jewish tradition it was during this time of year that God created the world, and so it will be this time that He will judge the world (b.*Rosh HaShanah* 27a).[27]

Yom Teruah/Rosh HaShanah has been honored in the past, and is honored today as a holiday, when we remember God and we acknowledge the fact that we are His people and we can convene together. It is a time where the *shofar* (שׁוֹפָר) or ram's horn is traditionally blown to commemorate the work of God, and call His people together. As Messianic Believers, we assemble to hear the *shofar* blown, and convene together as we prepare ourselves for the even more serious Day of Atonement.

Rosh HaShanah is a festival which many Christians are familiar with. They are familiar with it because many prophecy teachers, both pre-tribulational and post-tribulational alike, believe that Yeshua will return on this day to gather the saints, because of the simple reason that the trumpet is blown on this day. They compare the *shofar* blown to the trumpet blown in Second Coming passages such as Matthew 24:29-31, 1 Corinthians 15:51-52, and 1 Thessalonians 4:16-17. But contrary to popular belief, the Messiah will not gather the saints into the clouds on

---

[26] *BDB*, 929.

[27] It is commonly thought in much of today's independent Messianic quarters that the practice of remembering *Rosh HaShanah* on the first of Tishri was a pagan error that the Jewish exiles picked up in Babylon. This is not based in an accurate understanding of history, or of the Scriptures, but is often rooted in the conclusions of a Higher Criticism that dates the composition of the Pentateuch not to the time of Moses, but the post-exilic era. Consult the FAQ on the Messianic Apologetics website "Rosh HaShanah."

Yom Teruah/Rosh HaShanah and then return seven years later to judge the world at *Yom Kippur*. The resurrection will take place, the saints will be gathered to meet Him on *Yom Teruah*, and immediately following the wrath of God will be poured out on the world, culminating in the Battle of Armageddon.[28]

What must we remember on *Yom Teruah/Rosh HaShanah?* Obviously, we must come together in a holy convocation and hear the *shofar* blown. We do this because the LORD is God and He is Ruler of the Universe. We are called to remember that Yeshua is the Messiah and Redeemer, and we praise Him for who He is and what He has done for us. We convene and stand in the awe of God, because we are His people. We acknowledge how Yeshua is coming to fulfill the Fall appointed times sometime in the future, and gather us into His presence at the blowing of the trumpet.

The Day of Atonement/*Yom Kippur*

The time period between *Yom Teruah/Rosh HaShanah* and *Yom Kippur* is commonly known as the Ten Days of Awe—when the community of God's faithful prepares itself to corporately confess and repent of sin. The Day of Atonement is considered **to be the holiest day** on the Jewish calendar. The Torah specifies,

"The LORD spoke to Moses, saying, 'On exactly the tenth day of this seventh month is the day of atonement; it shall be a holy convocation for you, and you shall humble your souls and present an offering by fire to the LORD. You shall not do any work on this same day, for it is a day of atonement, to make atonement on your behalf before the LORD your God'" (Leviticus 23:26-28).

Just as many Christians are familiar with the Festival of Trumpets, many of the same are familiar with *Yom Kippur* (יוֹם כִּפּוּר) or the Day of Atonement, if for any other reason that they know that this is the one day of the year when Jews fast. *Yom Kippur* is to be a day when God's people are commanded to "afflict" themselves, usually by fasting, and by spending the day before Him. They should be individually confessing their sins of the previous year, making peace with anyone who has been wronged, and meditating on the future.

The Day of Atonement was the only time when the high priest was really permitted to go into the Holy of Holies and spread the sacrificial blood upon the Ark of the Covenant for covering the sin of the people (Leviticus 16). Following the Southern Kingdom's exile to Babylon, *Yom Kippur* was considered the only appropriate time that God's Divine Name was to be spoken aloud—and that was in the Temple alone (m.*Yoma* 6:2).

---

[28] For a further analysis, consult the author's publication *The Dangers of Pre-Tribulationism.*

Within Judaism, *Yom Kippur* is to be a very serious time of spiritual reflection. Hertz elaborates, "Confession of sin is the most essential and characteristic element in the services of the Day of Atonement; 'every one entreating pardon for his sins and hoping for God's mercy, not because of his own merits but through the compassionate nature of that Being who will have forgiveness rather than punishment' (Philo).[29] The confession is made by the whole Community collectively; and those who have not themselves committed the sins mentioned in the confession regret that they were unable to prevent them from being committed by others (Friedländer)."[30]

In recent days within the evangelical Christian community, there has been a substantial amount of discussion on the need for repentance and reconciliation with God. *This is good.* Many of the movements which have arisen have had some limited success for a season, but then fade away or lose their impact for some reason or another. While we as individuals should always be in the process of spiritual reflection, the simple truth of the matter is that there is a Biblical time when required corporate repentance and reconciliation with God are to take place: *Yom Kippur.* This is the day that the Body of Messiah is to entreat the Lord for mercy, as it involves fasting and traditional liturgy that *really is* designed to get people to think about their sins.[31]

Furthermore, concerning *Yom Kippur*, Leviticus 23:29-30 describes how "If there is any person who will not humble himself on this same day, he shall be cut off from his people. As for any person who does any work on this same day, that person I will destroy from among his people." The severity of the Day of Atonement cannot be overemphasized here. Those who did not humble and afflict themselves and abstain from work (in ancient times) would literally be cut off. The Hebrew verb is *karat* (כָּרַת), and generally means to be "cut off, cut down" (*BDB*).[32] The *ArtScroll Chumash* actually says, "one who works on Yom Kippur, about whom the Torah says he will be destroyed, is judged more harshly than one who eats, about whom the Torah says only that he will be cut off. One who eats is treated more leniently, because he is merely a glutton who cannot control his desires, but one who works shows that he is contemptuous of God's wishes."[33]

As Believers in Messiah Yeshua, we need to learn to take *Yom Kippur* very seriously. The Day of Atonement is intended to be a very serious and sober time. It is to be a time when we are reminded of our

---

[29] Philo *The Special Laws* 2.196.

[30] Hertz, 523.

[31] Consult the order of worship seen in "A Traditional Morning Service for Yom Kippur," appearing in the *Messianic Fall Holiday Helper* by Messianic Apologetics.

[32] *BDB*, 503.

[33] Scherman, *Chumash*, 687.

humanity before a holy and righteous Creator. It is to be a time when we are to reflect and confess sin. As members of the Commonwealth of Israel, Jewish or non-Jewish, we each must be reminded, in the words of Hertz, that "No other nation, ancient or modern, has an institution approaching the Day of Atonement in religious depth—'a day of purification and of turning from sins, for which forgiveness is granted through the grace of the merciful God, who holds penitence in as high as esteem as guiltlessness' (Philo)."[34]

Sadly, it has been our family observation over the years that a few in the Messianic community do not take *Yom Kippur* as seriously as they should. Part of this comes because these Messianics do not really know what to do about spiritual introspection. Many Christians today believe that since they have been forgiven of their sin through Yeshua, that it is unnecessary for them to ever ask for any forgiveness of sin again once they have been converted. They really do not see any importance in *Yom Kippur*, and in the need of taking a yearly spiritual inventory, and so some of today's Messianics have the same attitude and do not take *Yom Kippur* very seriously. This, I believe, is a very immature attitude because Paul teaches plainly, "work out your salvation with fear and trembling" (Philippians 2:12). We should always evaluate where we stand before Him at least once a year.

Yom Kippur is not just a day when we abstain from eating and the usual pleasures; it is to truly be the time when we are to stand in fear of an Eternal God. In no way are we to have a cavalier attitude about it, where one is "counting down the hours" left before breaking the required fast of the day. Many of us have to learn to take our salvation more seriously—or at least fast and pray for the salvation of others. Even if you think that you are right with God and that you have no business yourself to conduct with Him, there are lost people all over the world—especially our unsaved Jewish brethren—whom we should be fasting and interceding for!

As far as *Yom Kippur's* eschatological fulfillment is concerned, a future Day of Atonement will probably be the time when the Day of the LORD occurs, that being the time when God's wrath (Grk. *orgē*) is poured out upon the unsaved of Planet Earth and Yeshua defeats His enemies at Armageddon.

This concept is readily emphasized in the Tanach in the various Day of the LORD prophecies. "Wail, for the day of the LORD is near! It will come as destruction from the Almighty...Behold, the day of the LORD is coming, cruel, with fury and burning anger, to make the land a desolation; and He will exterminate its sinners from it...Therefore I will make the heavens tremble, and the earth will be shaken from its place

---

[34] Hertz, 523.
Cf. Philo *Special Laws* 1.229.

at the fury of the LORD of hosts in the day of His burning anger" (Isaiah 13:6, 9, 13). We are told in Ezekiel 30:3: "For the day is near, even the day of the LORD is near; it will be a day of clouds, a time *of doom* for the nations."

There are numerous other references in Scripture to this horrible time, each of which speaks in some way of "the day of the LORD's anger" (Zephaniah 2:2). In its largest Biblical context, the Day of the LORD is a very short period of time (even though the terminology can be used to describe the force of God's vindication). The prophetic fulfillment of *Yom Kippur* is probably best understood to represent this coming Day of the LORD, as the Day of Atonement is to be considered a very solemn, serious occasion between oneself and the Lord for reflection. *Yom Kippur* is to be a day of mourning, and the Scriptures tell us that at Yeshua's appearing to defeat His enemies, "all the tribes of the earth will mourn" (Matthew 24:30; Revelation 1:7).

We Messianics must observe *Yom Kippur* each year by afflicting ourselves and standing in awe of a holy, righteous, and Eternal God. We must take this day very seriously and confess our sin before the Lord, claiming the blood of Messiah Yeshua, and dedicating ourselves to His service for the next year. All too often, on the Day of Atonement we are reminded of how really human we are before our Creator and how much we must be humbled. It reminds us of God's future judgment on the world when many will say, "who shall be able to stand?" (Revelation 6:17, KJV).

Yom Kippur is to be a time of severity and it is an appropriate time for us to remember Yeshua's triumph over sin, death, and Satan. It would be good for the Messianic community if we started emphasizing the events of the coming Day of the LORD at *Yom Kippur* as well, when we might read the Scripture passages of the judgment of the world that is prophesied—so that we might really pray and intercede for the salvation of the lost:

"But who can endure the day of His coming? And who can stand when He appears? For He is like a refiner's fire and like fullers' soap" (Malachi 3:2).

Tabernacles/*Sukkot*

The final of the major appointed times occurs five days after *Yom Kippur:*

"Again the LORD spoke to Moses, saying, 'Speak to the sons of Israel, saying, "On the fifteenth of this seventh month is the Feast of Booths for seven days to the LORD. On the first day is a holy convocation; you shall do no laborious work of any kind. For seven days you shall present an offering by fire to the LORD. On the eighth day you shall have a holy convocation and present an offering by fire to the LORD; it is an assembly. You shall do no laborious work"'" (Leviticus 23:33-36).

Following *Yom Kippur* is *Sukkot* (סֻכּוֹת) or the Feast of Booths, also called the Feast of Tabernacles. Leviticus 23:42-43 instructed how during *Sukkot*, "You shall live in booths for seven days; all the native-born in Israel shall live in booths, so that your generations may know that I had the sons of Israel live in booths when I brought them out from the land of Egypt. I am the LORD your God." This was to be in remembrance of the time when the Lord led the Ancient Israelites out of Egypt and when they would build *sukkah*s (pl. *sukkot*) or temporary dwelling places, described by Hertz as being "a hastily-constructed and unsubstantial edifice."[35]

Sukkot, along with the Feast of Unleavened Bread and *Shavuot*, is one of the three pilgrimage festivals (Deuteronomy 16:16). Today, there are varying ways that Messianic Believers observe *Sukkot*. A few make the sincere effort to go to Israel and to Jerusalem during the feast and assemble with other Believers from all over the world. For those who are unable to go because of financial constraints, which is most, many celebrations take place at local assemblies where a congregational *sukkah* is built, usually from a wooden frame covered in palm branches or other "leafy" branches in remembrance of the temporary dwellings of the Israelites in the wilderness. Many choose to erect a *sukkah* in their backyards as they celebrate *Sukkot* with their families.

There is, of course, even more significance represented by *Sukkot*, especially for us as Believers and its relation to prophecy and to Yeshua. In Exodus 25:8 the Lord declares, "Let them construct a sanctuary for Me, that I may dwell among them." This verse establishes the foundational principle of *Sukkot*: God dwelling in the midst of human beings. We know that this element of our faith is realized fully in Messiah Yeshua, who "became flesh, and did tabernacle among us" (John 1:14, YLT), as God's presence was manifest via a human body, beyond Him just filling the Temple. But at the same time, we eagerly

---

[35] Ibid., 525.

cry out "Come quickly Lord Yeshua!" so that we might see the Messiah manifested in all His glory here on Earth in His Kingdom.

In a similar manner as the Tabernacle and the booths were to be "temporary" dwelling places in the wilderness, so will the Messiah's manifestation on Earth in His Kingdom after the Tribulation period be "temporary," so to speak. We emphasize "temporary" here because the Seventieth Week of Israel spiritually represents our trek from Egypt or *this world* to eternity. Yeshua's Millennial Kingdom is but an "intermediate time" before we see the New Heavens and the New Earth and the New Jerusalem—the New Creation God is preparing for us in eternity. We know this to be the case because in Jeremiah 31:38 when God restores Israel's Kingdom, that "the city will be rebuilt for the LORD from the Tower of Hananel to the Corner Gate," which occurs during the Millennium, versus the New Jerusalem which comes down from the sky (Revelation 21:2, 10).

Sukkot is a time when we are to concentrate on our Heavenly Father and His earnest desire to live among us. When Yeshua physically returns to the Earth, all people will be seriously mandated to observe the Feast of Tabernacles. Zechariah 14:16-17 describes how those who, during the Millennium, do not go to Jerusalem to honor the Feast of Tabernacles, will not receive any rain from the Lord: "Then it will come about that any who are left of all the nations that went against Jerusalem will go up from year to year to worship the King, the LORD of hosts, and to celebrate the Feast of Booths. And it will be that whichever of the families of the earth does not go up to Jerusalem to worship the King, the LORD of hosts, there will be no rain on them." So for some reason or another, some will not understand the concept of *communing* with the Lord.

The festival of *Sukkot* will likewise experience prophetic fulfillment at the end of the Millennium, as the Apostle John attests, "I heard a loud voice from the throne, saying, 'Behold, the tabernacle of God is among men, and He will dwell among them, and they shall be His people, and God Himself will be among them, and He will wipe away every tear from their eyes; and there will no longer be *any* death; there will no longer be *any* mourning, or crying, or pain; the first things have passed away'" (Revelation 21:3-4).

Sukkot or the Feast of Tabernacles is a wonderful holiday that the Lord is restoring to His people. *Sukkot* is a time when Messianic Believers are being drawn to the Lord and His desire to have our fellowship tabernacling with Him. They get to experience such a fellowship in a very tangible way, communing with Him and with others in their congregational or home *sukkahs*.[36]

---

[36] For resources on how to keep the Fall festivals with your family, consult the *Messianic Fall Holiday Helper* by Messianic Apologetics.

How do we honor the appointed times/*moedim*?

In this article, we have only briefly touched on each one of the appointed times of the Lord; there is certainly more that can be considered, much of which comes every successive year that they are remembered. What we have tried to do here is simply explain the importance of each one of these celebrations for us as Messianic Believers, the spiritual renewal that God is bringing to us by keeping them, and how the work of Yeshua is reflected in each holiday.

Many of us come from diverse religious backgrounds, be those backgrounds Jewish or Christian; liberal or conservative; Protestant, Catholic or Pentecostal. In particular for Messianic Believers from Christian backgrounds—each of whom has had a different "Christian experience," so too must we recognize that each Messianic congregation, family, and individual will celebrate the *moedim* a little differently. Some people will have more of a "Jewish" flavor to their celebration than others, and some will choose to have as little "Jewishness" as possible. How do we get the most out of the appointed times, so that our observance is focused on the Lord, and is also fulfilling?

There are many good Jewish traditions associated with the *moedim*, which are edifying to the Body of Messiah. Then again, there are Jewish traditions associated with these holidays that are not Biblical and that can take us away from the Messiah. I trust that you will seek balance and fairness in this regard. It is not prudent at all to simply reject everything (Orthodox) Jewish *carte blanche*, but then at the same time accept everything Jewish *carte blanche* either. If the Lord is truly reuniting restoring all His people, then those things that the Synagogue has contributed which are consistent with Scripture and spiritually uplifting **should be practiced**, and our Jewish brethren should be appropriately honored. But like all things, exhibit caution and discernment (cf. Philippians 4:8).

Ultimately, however you choose to celebrate the festivals of the Lord is up to you, but please leave leeway and grace for those who may not celebrate them exactly as you do. Let us remember that we are all on the road and we are all learning together.

The Restoration of the Appointed Times in His Kingdom

We are very excited that God's people are rediscovering His appointed times. It is a part of the prophesied "restoration of all things" (Acts 3:21) and a return to the way that our Father originally intended. Once we all start to celebrate His holidays on an annual basis, then we can adequately prepare ourselves for Yeshua's coming Kingdom where the *moedim* will be restored. Concerning the Levites and the Messianic Age, we are told,

"Moreover, they shall teach My people *the difference* between the holy and the profane, and cause them to discern between the unclean and the clean. In a dispute they shall take their stand to judge; they shall judge it according to My ordinances. They shall also keep My laws and My statutes in all My appointed feasts and sanctify My sabbaths" (Ezekiel 44:23-24).

If we are to truly be ruling and reigning with the Messiah during the Millennium, when God's Torah will be enforced as the Instruction for the whole Earth—then it is high time that we all start becoming familiar with His appointed times! The Levites will surely be keeping them as God's officials and judges.

Remembering *God's* Appointed Times

Many Christians do struggle with the issue of keeping the Lord's appointed times or *moedim,* either by wanting to act as though they were important only for a previous time, or they keep them at a spiritual arm's length. Yet, it is undeniable that one of the significant ways that today's Messianic movement has utterly ballooned in number, is because evangelical Believers have been drawn to the richness of keeping the appointed times in Messiah Yeshua. Others have noticed this, and have not been too positive in their assessment of it. Consider the following quote by author Tim Warner, a fundamentalist Christian, of The Last Trumpet website. He says the following in his article "Christians, and the Feasts of Israel":

> "Lets [sic] get one thing straight right up front. Keeping the Feasts according to the Torah <u>REQUIRES OFFERING ANIMAL SACRIFICES</u>. There is no avoiding this conclusion. And, any changes to the festivals by rabbis to accommodate the fact that there is no longer a Tabernacle/Temple or Levitical priesthood, or, any changes by Messianic Christians to accommodate the fact that the New Testament says Christ's sacrifice has ended the animal sacrifices, makes it impossible to observe these feasts according to the Torah."[37]

Warner is correct in asserting that we cannot perfectly observe the appointed times according to the Torah. The *moedim* do require animal sacrifices, and because there is no Temple in which to perform these sacrifices, we cannot keep them one-hundred percent correctly. But what is the position of many Christians because of this? *They reject the celebration of the Lord's appointed times entirely*. Warner might be

---

[37] Tim Warner (2002). *Christians, and the Feasts of Israel. The Last Trumpet.* Retrieved 06 January, 2003 from <http://www.lasttrumpet.com>.

exceptional when he says, "Does this mean the Feasts of Israel are of no value anymore? Quite the contrary. They are still witnesses to the gospel, in graphic allegory. They are rich in symbolism, and should be studied by all Christians, for a fuller understanding of the atonement of Christ, and how it relates to prophecy."[38] But, he also says, "Should Christians observe the Feasts? Yes, and no. Yes, if it is being done simply as a memorial, and instruction on the basis of our faith. No, if it is done out of obligation or necessity."[39]

If you can read between the lines of these statements, many Christians are opposed to any "mandatory" memorial of God's appointed times being observed by born again Believers. The idea that is really being purported here is that because we cannot perfectly observe the Lord's appointed times, because they require animal sacrifices which cannot be offered, is that we should really not try to keep them in any capacity at all. While it is true that the Jewish Rabbis over the centuries have added traditions to the holidays to compensate for the required animal sacrifices—mostly in the form of liturgical prayers—Christianity by-and-large has decided to totally dispense with the Lord's appointed times.

Which is worse: to augment your celebration and do the best that you can given your circumstances—recognizing that God is indeed gracious and merciful? Or, deciding to replace what God has asked His people to remember with something totally different and to do what you want? This, sadly, is what Christianity has often done. Judaism, even with some errors, at least has been trying to honor God in this area.

But this will not stop all Christians from speaking against the Lord's appointments. Consider the following admonishment from the Prophet Isaiah:

"'What are your multiplied sacrifices to Me?' says the LORD. 'I have had enough of burnt offerings of rams and the fat of fed cattle; and I take no pleasure in the blood of bulls, lambs or goats. When you come to appear before Me, who requires of you this trampling of My courts? Bring your worthless offerings no longer, incense is an abomination to Me. New moon and sabbath, the calling of assemblies—I cannot endure iniquity and the solemn assembly. I hate your new moon *festivals* and your appointed feasts, they have become a burden to Me; I am weary of bearing *them.* So when you spread out your hands *in prayer,* I will hide My eyes from you; yes, even though you multiply prayers, I will not listen. Your hands are covered with blood. Wash yourselves, make yourselves clean; remove the evil of your deeds from My sight. Cease to

---

[38] Ibid.
[39] Ibid.

do evil, learn to do good; seek justice, reprove the ruthless, defend the orphan, plead for the widow" (Isaiah 1:11-17).

Many of you who have read this text know how it has been misapplied.[40] Here the Lord speaks of how He was displeased with how the Southern Kingdom was celebrating His feasts and appointments. He specifically said, "I hate all your festivals and sacrifices. I cannot stand the sight of them!" (Isaiah 1:14, NLT). Many Christians have interpreted this as meaning that the Lord was tired with *His* feast days and wanted to get rid of them, but this is not what the text says at all. The text specifically says "I hate **your** new moon *festivals* and **your** appointed feasts [*chodshei'khem u'moadei'khem*, חָדְשֵׁיכֶם וּמוֹעֲדֵיכֶם]." Specifically, what God is saying is that He could not stand how the people were celebrating *His* feasts, and so He called them "**your** New Moons and **your** appointed times" (ATS), putting the responsibility on the people for the wrong they have done.

God placing the burden of proof on His people is not something unique to the Tanach. In Exodus 32:7 He told Moses, "Go down; for **your** people [*amekha*, עַמְּךָ], whom **you** brought up out of the land of Egypt, have corrupted themselves." As Moses reminded the Lord, "O LORD, why does **Your** anger burn against **Your people** whom **You** have brought out from the land of Egypt with great power and with a mighty hand?" (Exodus 32:11), indicating that although the people have sinned against Him, He was still the One who led them out of Egypt.

Similarly, the appointed times ordained by God in the Torah, *are still His.* Recognizing that people have improperly used His appointed times in the past is recognized by John A. Martin in the *Bible Knowledge Commentary: Old Testament*, edited by dispensational theologians John F. Walvoord and Roy B. Zuck of Dallas Theological Seminary:

"Isaiah's point is that the people assumed that merely by offering sacrifices at the altar they would be made ceremonially clean before God. Even multiple sacrifices are **meaningless** (v. 13) and therefore do not please God when the 'worshiper' does not bring his life into conformity with God's standards. Also the careful observance of monthly **offerings**...were **meaningless** to God when they were not

---

[40] Isaiah 1:11-17 was most especially misapplied by Tertullian, where he says "The Holy Spirit upbraids the Jews with their holy-days. 'Your Sabbaths, and new moons, and ceremonies,' says He, 'My soul hateth'" (*On Idolatry* 14).

Even more problematic is Tertullian's conclusion, based on Paul's words in 1 Corinthians 10:32-33 about him not unnecessarily being an offense, that "No doubt he used to please them by celebrating the Saturnalia and New-year's day!" This is an extrapolation that the good Apostle would not have supported (cf. 2 Corinthians 6:14).

Cf. "Sabbath," in David W. Bercot, ed., *A Dictionary of Early Christian Beliefs* (Peabody, MA: Hendrickson, 1998), 572.

done with the proper attitude....Such observances God called **evil** because they were carried out hypocritically, with sinful hearts."[41]

Indeed, if our remembrance of the Lord's appointed times is not from the heart, and is only outward, then our celebration of the appointed times could not mean that much. Sadly, there are Messianics who fit this category all too well, because they use every festival season as a time to unfairly criticize and harass our Christian brothers and sisters who do not celebrate them—rather than inviting people to their homes and fellowships to join with them, so that they might be blessed. But then in total fairness, there are Christians who celebrate non-Biblical holidays and festivals—consciously rejecting and spurning His appointed times, *thinking they are honoring the Lord.* Are they truly honoring Him by rejecting what He has laid out in His Word? Thankfully, He is the One who knows the heart, and the ultimate determination is up to Him and not any mortal.

We need to honor the Lord's appointed times, both outwardly in our congregations and assemblies, and inwardly in our hearts because we have a sincere desire to obey Him. We need to understand His plan of salvation history in a more profound way, and via our proper remembrance, see others drawn to us by the wooing of the Spirit.

---

[41] John A. Martin, "Isaiah," in John F. Walvoord and Roy B. Zuck, eds., *The Bible Knowledge Commentary, Old Testament* (Wheaton, IL: Victor Books, 1985), pp 1035-1036.

Does the New Testament Annul the Biblical Appointments?

We as Messianic Believers need to lament over the fact that most of our Christian brothers and sisters do not honor and observe our Heavenly Father's appointed times[1] or *moedim* (מוֹעֲדִים),[2] listed in Leviticus 23. Instead of remembering *Pesach*/Passover, *Chag HaMatzot*/Unleavened Bread, *Shavuot*/Pentecost, *Yom Teruah-Rosh HaShanah*/the Feast of Trumpets, *Yom Kippur*/the Day of Atonement, *Sukkot*/Tabernacles, and *Shemini Atzeret*/the Eighth Day Assembly, in addition to the weekly seventh-day *Shabbat*/Sabbath—Christians today celebrate Christmas and Easter and assemble on Sunday. They have missed out on much of what the Lord has to show us, by avoiding to meet when He wants to meet with His people. Certainly, if anyone is truly committed to God and wants to honor and celebrate Him as much as possible, the advantage of remembering His appointed times over various human replacements is obvious. Eight appointed times versus two holidays and about two hours on Sunday. *It is obvious by the numbers alone that what He intended is better!*

All too often, we as Messianics can be unfairly chastised by Christians for wanting to obey the Lord by observing His appointments. It is not uncommon to be called legalistic for celebrating the Biblical festivals. In fact, some say that we are going too far, or are perhaps

---

[1] This article is reproduced from the author's book *Torah In the Balance, Volume I* (Kissimmee, FL: TNN Press, 2003/2009).

[2] The Hebrew term *moedim* (מוֹעֲדִים) is translated variably as "appointed times" (NASU), "appointed feasts" (NIV), "fixed times" (NJPS), and "appointed festivals" (ATS). CHALOT defines the singular *moed* (מוֹעֵד) as "**meeting assembly**," and "**appointed time, fixed day**," indicating that it is used in the Tanach for the "**tent of meeting**" where the elders of Israel met with the Lord (p 186).

trying to earn our salvation, and in a few cases that we are not even saved. These claims against us are completely unacceptable if we are reasonable Believers united around a common hope of salvation in Messiah Yeshua (Christ Jesus).[3] There is nothing wrong with obeying God or His Word and in following the instructions that He has laid out for us. By remembering the Biblical appointments, we as Messianic Believers are following the example of our Messiah Yeshua and the early First Century Jewish Apostles and Believers who likewise observed them as a part of their faith practice.

Contrary to popular opinion, the First Century Apostles and Believers did not celebrate "Christmas" or "Easter," or even a "Sunday Sabbath"—especially as we know them today. They observed the *moedim* of Leviticus 23 and the weekly *Shabbat*,[4] and on these special days remembered who Messiah Yeshua was as the Savior of Israel. As James the Just attested to the Apostle Paul, "You see, brother, how many thousands there are among the Jews of those who have believed, and they are all zealous for the Law" (Acts 21:20). Now, the same is being said of many non-Jewish Believers who likewise have faith in Yeshua and who are zealous for the things of God's Torah, eagerly partaking of their heritage in Israel (Ephesians 3:6). God is bringing all of His people together in a very unique and special way.

But there are those who say otherwise. There are those who say that because of Yeshua's sacrifice at Golgotha (Calvary), the Torah or Law of Moses has been abolished, and thus the *moedim* or appointed times are likewise done away with, annulled, and abolished. Some think that they might be important for us to study for understanding the Bible in an historical sense, but are not to be followed as standard elements of our orthopraxy.[5] Others think that by remembering things like the Passover, we have actually turned our heads away from Yeshua, and bring dishonor to Him as our final sacrifice. Those who frown on Messianics keeping the appointed times, regardless of the degree of how strong they speak against them, or frown upon them, say that the Apostle Paul gave us specific instruction in his epistles that we are no longer to celebrate the "Old Testament holidays."

---

[3] Cf. Ephesians 4:1-6.

[4] Consider varied references in the Apostolic Scriptures to *Shavuot*/Pentecost (Acts 20:16; 1 Corinthians 16:8) and *Yom Kippur*/the Day of Atonement, "the fast" (Acts 27:9). Why would these holidays even be referenced if the Believers in the First Century were not observing them to some degree? Furthermore, Acts 17:2 tells us that it was Paul's custom to go to the local synagogue on the Sabbath day *first*, when he went into a new community, to reason with those assembled to present them with the gospel.

[5] The term "orthopraxy" "literally [means] 'right practice,'...living out the known and experienced truth in the Christian faith in love and justice" (Stanley J. Grenz, David Guretzki, and Cherith Fee Nordling, *Pocket Dictionary of Theological Terms* [Downers Grove, IL: InterVarsity, 1999], 94). For our purposes as Messianics, it means how our faith is to be properly lived out and how Torah observance is practiced in the world.

Do the Apostolic Scriptures (New Testament) truly tell us not to celebrate the Biblical holidays? Are the Biblical holidays no longer of any value to us as Believers? **What might a closer reading of the Biblical text reveal?**

It is important that we examine the three common Scripture passages (Galatians 4:9-11; Colossians 2:16-17; Romans 14:5-6) which are often given to support the premise that Believers today are not supposed to remember the *moedim* or appointed times of the Torah, placing them in proper context.[6] These words were originally given to distinct ancient audiences with some specific issues facing *them,* and not necessarily Twenty-First Century people. Knowing that Yeshua the Messiah upheld the validity of the Torah as a standard for good works (Matthew 5:16-19), and that remembering the appointed times is a simple matter of outward obedience, is it possible to see how the majority view out there has missed some things? Let us read these verses and investigate their background a bit more fully.

Galatians 4:9-11

"But now that you have come to know God, or rather to be known by God, how is it that you turn back again to the weak and worthless elemental things, to which you desire to be enslaved all over again? You observe days and months and seasons and years. I fear for you, that perhaps I have labored over you in vain."

These verses, from Paul's Epistle to the Galatians, are part of a grossly misunderstood letter that is often not interpreted by Christian laypersons in light of Yeshua's words regarding: (1) the fact that the relevance of the Torah still stands (Matthew 5:17-19), (2) the later Jerusalem Council ruling of Acts 15:19-21 of how the non-Jews coming to faith were anticipated to go to the local synagogue and hear Moses' Teaching,[7] and (3) that the Galatians were relatively new Believers who were being (easily) led astray by outsiders using a position of perceived importance to exert ungodly influences.

---

[6] I have chosen to address these passages in the order of frequency in which Messianic Believers often hear them quoted, *not* their order of composition (Galatians-Romans-Colossians).

[7] Acts 15:21 specifically says, "For Moses from ancient generations has in every city those who preach him, since he is read in the synagogues every Sabbath." This verse appears after the non-Jewish Believers in Antioch are told to "abstain from things contaminated by idols and from fornication and from what is strangled and from blood" (Acts 15:20), concepts deeply rooted in the Torah (Exodus 3:15-17; Leviticus 18:6-23; 3:17; 7:26; 17:10, 14; 19:26; Deuteronomy 12:16, 23; 15:23). These were the four minimum requirements to be observed for the new non-Jewish Believers to interact with the Jewish community, where in the local synagogue they could be exposed to the Torah and Tanach.

For a more detailed discussion, consult the author's commentary *Acts 15 for the Practical Messianic.*

How are people to be reckoned as a part of God's covenant community? Why did outside influences sneak in, once Paul had finished his ministry activity in Galatia (Acts 13:13-14:28), requiring him to issue a sharp rebuke? What were some of the specific things warned against?

It can be very easy without any background information, both from other Scripture passages and from Ancient Galatia, to misinterpret Paul's words. While it is rightfully thought that the Galatian false teaching was that many of the Galatians were being told that strict obedience to the Law and circumcision would bring them salvation and inclusion among God's people, as proselyte converts—the common conclusion that Paul's letter is a treatise against the relevance of God's Torah for born again Believers is simply not true. Paul clearly asserts in Galatians 3:21, "Is the Law then contrary to the promises of God? May it never be!"

Rather, Paul's letter is a clarification of how various doings are not to be considered as a way of salvation and inclusion among God's people—actually placed over and against faith in God! One's justification is not to be found in any human or sectarian "works of law" (cf. 4QMMT),[8] but instead "through the faithfulness of Yeshua the Messiah" (my translation)[9]—meaning His obedience to the Father unto death on our behalf (Galatians 2:16). From such a revelation of what Yeshua has done, proper obedience to the Lord was to come forth.

Placing one's trust in what Yeshua has accomplished for us is a major overriding theme of Galatians. Yet, because of some misinterpretations of Paul's letter to the Galatians—and specifically for

---

[8] Grk. *ergōn nomou* (ἔργων νόμου).

Consult the author's article "What Are 'Works of the Law'?" for a further discussion, especially with how modern Pauline scholarship has made connections between *ergōn nomou* and the *ma'sei haTorah* (מעשי התורה) appearing in the Dead Sea Scrolls. The latter defined "works of law" composed the sectarian identity markers of the Qumran community, and would thus have been various doings that defined the Judaizers'/Influencers' sect of Judaism. "Works of law" in Galatians would not necessarily be "observing the law" (NIV), but how the Torah was applied in a particular sectarian way, perhaps even contrary to the imperatives of written Scripture (Galatians 3:10; cf. Deuteronomy 27:26).

For a broader view in contemporary scholarship, also consult T.R. Schreiner, "Works of the Law," in Gerald F. Hawthorne, Ralph P. Martin, and Daniel G. Reid, eds., *Dictionary of Paul and His Letters* (Downers Grove, IL: InterVarsity, 1993), pp 975-979; James W. Thompson, "Works," David Noel Friedman, ed., *Eerdmans Dictionary of the Bible* (Grand Rapids: Eerdmans, 2000), 1387; "deeds, works," in *Dictionary of Judaism in the Biblical Period*, 159.

[9] Grk. *dia pisteōs Iēsou Christou* (διὰ πίστεως Ἰησοῦ Χριστοῦ).

Consult the author's article "The Faithfulness of Yeshua the Messiah," evaluating various opinions as to whether an objective genitive (case indicating possession) "faith in Yeshua the Messiah," or a subjective genitive "faith(fulness) of Yeshua the Messiah," is used in Galatians 2:16, and other passages in the Pauline corpus.

failing to consider some of its significant First Century Jewish background—it is simply and wrongly thought that in Galatians 4:9-11 Paul desperately feared for the Galatians, because they actually began to remember the Biblical appointed times as laid out in the Law of Moses. Donald K. Campbell's thoughts on these verses in *The Bible Knowledge Commentary* are fairly typical of mainstream Christian opinions:

"Under the influence of the Judaizers the Galatians had at least begun to observe the Mosaic calendar. They kept special days (weekly sabbaths), and months (new moons), and seasons (seasonal festivals such as Passover, Pentecost, and Tabernacles), and years (sabbatical and jubilee years)....They observed these special times, thinking that they would thereby gain additional merit before God. But Paul had already made it clear that works could not be added to faith as grounds for either justification or sanctification."[10]

I certainly agree with the comment here that human works are not to be grounds for salvation, as salvation is a free gift of God available through Messiah Yeshua. "Keeping the feasts," as it were, will not gain a person eternal salvation. But the free gift of salvation does not negate the need for obedience, as obedience to God is to follow a true salvation experience, and I would disagree with the comment here that obeying His Torah should not be a part of the sanctification process. We learn about God's holiness by remembering the days He considers to be important.

The Galatians were not following the Torah as a part of the sanctification process. The non-Jewish Galatians were being errantly influenced by the Judaizers that their salvation had to be preceded by circumcision and Torah observance (and perhaps even observance of the Oral Law), being reckoned as ethnic Jews, and only then they could be a part of God's covenant people.

Paul's epistle was written concerning a serious situation in Galatia where these outsiders had sneaked in, and imposed strict legalisms on the non-Jewish Believers, leading them astray. While there is nothing wrong with physical circumcision in and of itself, nor is obeying the Torah wrong, doing these things with a legalistic attitude and improper motives will not bring eternal salvation. Only following the Torah the way that a particular Jewish sect prescribed—"works of law"—was certainly **not enough** to be reckoned as a part of His covenant people. **The Epistle to the Galatians establishes how covenant status with God has always been defined by faith in God, and now His Messiah** (Galatians 3:6; cf. Genesis 15:6).

Was Paul really concerned that the Galatians were being instructed by God's Law? Or was Paul concerned about *their motivations* for doing

---

[10] Donald K. Campbell, "Galatians," in John F. Walvoord and Roy B. Zuck, eds., *The Bible Knowledge Commentary: New Testament* (Wheaton, IL: Victor Books, 1983), 602.

what they were doing? Was the Galatians' attitude one of trying to grow via the natural pace of the Holy Spirit, or to prove themselves superior to others? What did the outside Judaizers/Influencers come in and really want them to do (cf. Galatians 6:12)?

Salvation only comes through being spiritually regenerated through the atoning work of Messiah Yeshua. Who we are in the Lord is because of what the Lord has done for us! After salvation, good works should follow and be *a natural evidence of the changes brought of the Holy Spirit* (Ezekiel 36:26-27). There are certainly some Messianics today who may teach, or by their actions demonstrate, that they believe that their human-prescribed works are necessary to precede salvation, rather than salvation preceding works—the same paradigm paralleled in Galatians. We are to heed Paul's words to the Galatians **so that we never fall into this trap.**

But what is Paul saying in Galatians 4:9-11? Is he telling his audience that they were falling away because they were keeping the appointed times of the Torah? Is he telling them that they were wrong to observe "The LORD's appointed times which" are "holy convocations" (Leviticus 23:2)? If the non-Jews coming to faith, later addressed in Acts 15, were anticipated to go to the local synagogue to hear Moses' Teaching—and indeed keeping the appointed times is a key element of following God's Torah—is there something that we have perhaps missed or glossed over? Even though this ruling came after Paul's letter was written to the Galatians, they would still have known about it and would have been expected to follow it.

In the text from Galatians, Paul prefaces his statements about the appointed times, by reminding his audience about their previous life:

"However at that time, when you did not know God, you were slaves to those which by nature are no gods. But now that you have come to know God, or rather to be known by God, how is it that you turn back again to the weak and worthless elemental things, to which you desire to be enslaved all over again?" (Galatians 4:8-9).

In v. 8 Paul describes the previous condition of the Galatians prior to coming to faith in the Messiah of Israel. He says that "you were in bondage to beings that by nature are no gods" (RSV). Now that they knew the God of Israel and the salvation of His Son, he asked them why they were returning "to the weak and worthless elementary principles of the world" (ESV).[11] The Greek verb *epistrephō* (ἐπιστρέφω), rendered as "turn back again" (NASU), means **"to return to a point where one has been, *turn around, go back*"** (BDAG).[12] This is a

---

[11] Grk. *ta asthenē kai ptōcha stoicheia* (τὰ ἀσθενῆ καὶ πτωχὰ στοιχεῖα).

[12] Frederick William Danker, ed., et. al., *A Greek-English Lexicon of the New Testament and Other Early Christian Literature*, third edition (Chicago: University of Chicago Press, 2000), 382.

good textual indicator that the Galatians were returning back to religious practices that were either (1) the exact same pagan practices that they followed before their conversion experience, or (2) practices that were similar in scope to the pagan ones that they followed before their conversion experience. Either way, they were turning to things that **were not of God.** There has to be a viable alternative explanation to the one that is often accepted.

To assert that these are the Lord's appointed times of Leviticus 23, and that Paul is equating Biblical practices and pagan practices as being quantitatively indifferent, would be to claim that things established by God *are not of God* but really of the world. Such logic is baffling and must be rejected.[13]

Samuel J. Mikolaski, in *The New Bible Commentary: Revised*, explains that in v. 8 the reference to "no gods" designates "celestial and demonic powers which control destiny, as in ancient astrology and mythology...the devotee was related to these as a slave, not like the Christian to the true God as a son. The elemental spirits are by nature excluded from being God, and were served only, because the Galatians did not formerly know God."[14] These words confirm that prior to the Galatians' knowing Yeshua they were practicing things that were not only not of God, but rooted in things like astrology and mythology, which were directly prohibited by the Torah (Leviticus 19:26; Deuteronomy 18:10). When the Galatians were returning back to their previous ways, these are the sorts of ways that they were returning to.

If indeed so, then what were the "days and months and seasons and years" (v. 10) referred to here? Are they the appointed times of God's Torah? Or, if the Galatians were returning to their previous ways left behind in Greco-Roman paganism, were these things something else? There are several possibilities. Ben Witherington III is keen to note how, "Commentators have often tried to parallel this list with various Jewish sources, but in fact there is no Jewish list that actually matches up with this list...Paul has provided here a generic list that could apply equally well to Jewish as well to pagan observances."[15] **Automatically**

---

[13] There are, sadly, Galatians commentators who do advocate this view. Richard N. Longenecker is one who actually concludes,

"[B]y taking on Torah observance Gentile Christians would be reverting to a pre-Christian stance comparable to their former pagan worship," and he goes on to say "Paul's lumping of Judaism and paganism together in this manner is radical in the extreme" (*Word Biblical Commentary: Galatians*, Vol. 41 [Nashville: Nelson Reference & Electronic, 1990], 181).

[14] Samuel J. Mikolaski, "Galatians," in D. Guthrie., et. al., *The New Bible Commentary: Revised* (Grand Rapids: Eerdmans, 1970), 1100.

[15] Ben Witherington III, *Grace in Galatia: A Commentary on Paul's Letter to the Galatians* (Grand Rapids: Eerdmans, 1998), 299.

Witherington does, though, believe that these are the Torah-prescribed appointed times.

assuming that Galatians 4:9-11 abolishes mainline Biblical practices is a bit too convenient, especially given what Paul says about the Galatians returning to things they were supposed to have left behind.

The first possibility is that what is being referred to are non-Biblical, pagan holidays. The foolish and young Galatians, falsely believing themselves to be securely saved by their circumcision and now a formal part of Judaism, could be returning to something like the Emperor Cult in order to maintain a connection to their non-believing extended family and the Greco-Roman community, and there are commentators who hold to this view.[16] A second, and I believe more likely possibility, is that "the days and months and seasons and years" involved fringe Jewish practices that were legalistically imposed by the Judaizers/Influencers, somehow similar to pagan Galatian practices, involving astrology or mysticism. They could actually be the standardized *moedim* or appointed times, yet infused with ungodly rituals that bore little difference to what the Galatians had previously observed prior to hearing the gospel. They were not God's "appointed times," per se, but rather the appointed times infused with pagan-influenced superstitions.

It is often easy for people today to overlook the fact that parts of Ancient Judaism had been influenced by the pagan world around it, and that there were aberrant branches of Judaism that made the spread of the gospel quite difficult for the Apostles (just consider the Jewish magician Elymas in Acts 13:6-12).[17] While speaking of the overall, fallen human condition in Galatians 4:3—"while we were children, [we] were held in bondage under the elemental things of the world"[18]—this *Zeitgeist* could affect Judaism equally as much as it could affect paganism. The historian Josephus attested how there were Pharisees and Essenes who both believed in the force known as Fate:

"Now for the Pharisees, they say that some actions, but not all, are the work of fate, and some of them are in our own power, and that they are liable to fate, but are not caused by fate. But the sect of the Essenes affirm, that fate governs all things, and that nothing befalls men but what is according to its determination" (*Antiquities of the Jews* 13.172).[19]

In ancient times, these "elemental things" or *stoicheia* (στοιχεῖα) were often considered to be forces like earth, water, air, and fire

---

[16] This is a position held by Mark D. Nanos, *The Irony of Galatians: Paul's Letter in First-Century Context* (Minneapolis: Fortress Press, 2002), pp 268-269; and Tim Hegg, *A Study of Galatians* (Tacoma, WA: TorahResource, 2002), pp 158-160.

[17] Elymas was someone Paul encountered immediately prior to his visit to Southern Galatia (Acts 13:13-14:28). It is possible that Paul, telling the Galatians about his previous travels, would have relayed his encounter with this magician to them.

[18] Grk. *ta stoicheia tou kosmou* (τὰ στοιχεῖα τοῦ κόσμου).

[19] Flavius Josephus: *The Works of Josephus: Complete and Unabridged*, trans. William Whiston (Peabody, MA: Hendrickson, 1987), 275.

(corresponding to the Greek deities Demeter, Poseidon, Hera, and Hephaestus),[20] or perhaps other elements such as the sun, moon, stars and/or spirits, angels, and demons (referred to in Romans 8:38 as "principalities"). The Jewish philosopher Philo was one who recognized the function of these *stoicheia* on the breastplate of the high priest:

"Now of the **three elements** [*stoicheiōn*, στοιχείων], out of which and in which all the different kinds of things which are perceptible by the outward senses and perishable are formed, namely, **the air, the water and the earth**, the garment which reached down to the feet in conjunction with the ornaments which were attached to that part of it which was about the ankles have been plainly shown to be appropriate symbols; for as the tunic is one, and as the aforesaid three elements are all of one species, since they all have all their revolutions and changes beneath the moon, and as to the garment are attached the pomegranates, and the flowers; so also in certain manner the earth and the water may be said to be attached to and suspended from the air, for the air is their chariot" (*Life of Moses* 2.121).[21]

Here, Philo, albeit errantly, concludes that the basic elements of the world—in which the pagans believed—functioned on the breastplate of the high priest. Similar to Fate controlling the destinies of people, these basic elements here communicated messages to the high priest of Israel.

Paul's remarks about the "the elemental things of the world" including not only aspects of First Century paganism, but also aspects of paganism that negatively influenced Judaism, seem likely. David H. Stern does point out, "Jews, though knowing the one true God, were sometimes led astray by demonic spirits."[22] Tim Hegg further explains, "This demonic 'worldview' had also influenced the Judaisms of the day, and had, to one extent or another, become the thinking of the common man, whether Jew or Gentile."[23]

---

[20] Cf. F.F. Bruce, *New International Greek Testament Commentary: Galatians* (Grand Rapids: Eerdmans, 1982), 193.

[21] Philo Judaeus: *The Works of Philo: Complete and Unabridged*, trans. C.D. Yonge (Peabody, MA: Hendrickson, 1993), 501.

[22] David H. Stern, *Jewish New Testament Commentary* (Clarksville, MD: Jewish New Testament Publications, 1995), 556.

[23] Tim Hegg, *A Study of Galatians* (Tacoma, WA: TorahResource, 2002), pp 142-143.
Hegg goes on to conclude that the "elemental things of the world" that had infected Judaism included elements of proto-Gnosticism that would later be seen in Medieval Jewish mysticism:

"If indeed a pre-Gnosticism was already extant in the Judaisms of Paul's day, he could well speak of being under the 'elemental principles of the world' when he considered the manner in which the rabbinic interpretations of the day had combined Hellenistic thought with the study of Torah. But for Paul, the Hellenistic concept of the *stoicheia* was not merely an errant form of philosophy—it was pagan and the realm of demons. Not unlike the kabbalism that would captivate Judaism in the middle-ages, the nascent Jewish Gnosticism in Paul's day was a mixing of things that essentially differ" (Ibid., 143).

Is it impossible to think that what the Galatians were actually practicing were pagan rituals that had infected the Judaizers/Influencers' (fringe) sect of Judaism? If they were, then what Paul spoke against was the Galatians observing the appointed times saturated with ungodly rituals—possibly involving Fate, astrology, or some kind of mysticism. Mikolaski's comments are well taken:

"Are these Jewish or pagan observances? In writing to the Galatians, Paul clearly has Judaizers in mind. Did these worship elemental spirits? Astrological elements were at times infused into Jewish as well as pagan practices. The *elemental spirits* of this age refer probably to the ethos of an age traceable in part to pagan astrological mythology, but which had become a religious habit as much as, and perhaps more than, a metaphysical system."[24]

This evangelical Christian commentator seems to imply that whatever days the Galatians were observing, the Judaizers could have integrated astrology into them. This being the case, Paul would have been deeply concerned that the Galatians were returning to the same kinds of practices that they followed in paganism. Paul's words, "I fear for you, that perhaps I have labored over you in vain" (Galatians 4:11), would certainly be justified in this regard. Likewise, his words that the Judaizers/Influencers did not even keep the Torah they claimed to uphold, even though they were insisting upon proselyte circumcision (cf. Galatians 6:13), also make much more sense. The Galatians needed to return to Paul's guidance, and the path established for them by Yeshua (cf. Galatians 5:1) for appropriate obedience.

Paul's concern for the Galatians adopting pagan practices that had influenced a fringe sect of Judaism—the sect of the Judaizers/Influencers—is highlighted by his opening warning in Galatians 1:8: "But even if we, or an angel from heaven, should preach to you a gospel contrary to what we have preached to you, he is to be accursed!" The *IVP Bible Background Commentary: New Testament* by

---

[24] Mikolaski, in *NBCR*, 1100.

Daniel C. Juster, *Jewish Roots* (Shippensburg, PA: Destiny Image, 1995), pp 114-115 draws a related conclusion:

"The full context has prompted many commentators to hold that Paul here is not speaking of Jewish biblical celebrations. There must have been another problem in Galatia, it is thought. This problem is acknowledged to be connected with astrology. It is also known that heretical groups existed which *connected some of the Jewish holidays to astrology* and superstition. Paul could not be speaking of celebrations given by God as putting people under the bondage of evil spirits! Nor could he be speaking of Jewish holidays in saying that they, a non-Jewish group, are *turning back* to weak and beggarly elemental spirits.

"Apparently, what Paul refers to is a drift into superstition connected to special years, days and seasons—akin to astrology. This is a bondage, for during such days, some actions are safe and others are unsafe, some endeavors are to be undertaken and will be especially fruitful, while others are especially dangerous. This actually brings bondage to evil spirits. There may have been a perverted Jewish content added to some of this."

Craig S. Keener, states, concerning Galatians 1:8, "Some Jewish mystics of the period claimed revelations from angels (especially in the *apocalyptic literature)…Paul may allude here to the curses of the covenant leveled against those who failed to keep Moses' law (Deut 27-28)."[25]

If the Judaizers who errantly influenced the Galatians were in fact some kind of Jewish mystics (the forerunners of practicing what we today call Kabbalah) practicing astrology, witchcraft, or some other kind of mysticism (cf. Deuteronomy 18:10-14; 2 Kings 21:6)—perhaps even claiming to have been given revelations by God—then of course Paul would be warning the Galatians that they had returned to the same worthless and God-less practices that they followed before acknowledging Yeshua. His question to them is, after all, "who has bewitched you?" (Galatians 3:1), which might be a little more literal than we commonly give it credit.[26] Remember how it is "days and months and seasons and years" (Galatians 4:10) that are targeted, pagan influences on Judaism which could have been super-imposed onto the appointed times. (Of course, if the Judaizers errantly influencing the Galatians were mystics is true, then some commonly held interpretations of Galatians should be reevaluated.)

The good Apostle who says that the Torah's main purpose is to lead people to the Messiah (Galatians 3:24), would not be speaking against the appointed times that depict the Father's plan of salvation history. Paul would speak against their misuse, though, as the Galatians were returning to various practices that would not have been approved by God. Paul is greatly concerned that the Galatians were turning to things not of the God of Israel, being enslaved to them. These cannot be the Biblical holidays because the appointed times are of God; they are certainly not "weak and miserable principles" (Galatians 4:9, NIV). They are the special times when our Heavenly Father wants His people to meet and fellowship with Him, so that He may reveal Himself fully to us. But if the appointed times were saturated with any mystical pagan practices by the outsiders who had led them astray—for that Paul would have been definitely concerned!

It is important to note that many Christians, whether they know it or not, unfortunately fall into the same errors as these Galatians. When many Christians come to faith in Messiah Yeshua, they turn to keeping "days and months and seasons and years" not established by God. Most of the time they do so in ignorance, failing to understand the theological

---

[25] Craig S. Keener, *IVP Bible Background Commentary: New Testament* (Downers Grove, IL: InterVarsity, 1999), 520.

[26] Witherington, *Galatians*, pp 201-202, notes how this could easily be some kind of connection to the ancient concept of the evil eye (Deuteronomy 28:54, LXX; Sirach 14:6, 8; Wisdom 4:12). The evil eye was used in sorcery and witchcraft.

and spiritual significance of the *moedim* given to us in the Torah. But then others, understanding the importance of the Lord's festivals, choose to say that they are not for today and are unimportant. And then, some Christians celebrate the utterly Satanic holiday of Halloween, and in spite of even the evidence against observing it compiled by evangelical Christian Bible teachers, still keep it.[27] The vast majority of Christians celebrate non-Biblical holidays. And a few, in spite of the richness that the Lord's appointed times have, defiantly refuse to honor them, and put others down who do. What do we do about this?

The Christians who criticize Messianics, saying that they are "concerned" because we honor God's appointments found in the Torah, probably need to read the verses they quote from Galatians a little closer and place them in proper historical context. They need to read these texts with a discerning eye. *What were the Galatians really returning to?* These verses may very well apply more to some of today's Christians than Messianic Believers, because today Christians observe holidays that were not established by God, but rather are human replacements for what He established. Thankfully in our day, the Lord is awakening many to the importance of His appointed times and many are indeed returning to His ways. People are seeing that what God has established for His people is better than anything that mortals can attempt to establish.[28]

Colossians 2:16-17

"Therefore no one is to act as your judge in regard to food or drink or in respect to a festival or a new moon or a Sabbath day—things which are a *mere* shadow of what is to come; but the substance belongs to Messiah."

This text from Paul's letter to the Colossians is often employed to demonstrate that no one is permitted to judge Believers in relation to "eating or in drinking, or in respect of a feast, or of a new moon, or of sabbaths" (YLT). These things, as Paul writes, are "only shadows of the real thing, Christ himself" (NLT). Those who think that the Biblical holidays of Leviticus 23, the seventh-day Sabbath, and kosher dietary laws, have been done away, often use Colossians 2:16-17 as a proof text.

While often considering observance of the appointed times to be an issue of personal preference or choice, many Christians who witness Messianics' observance of them, feel judged by the actions of us remembering the appointed times, even when we do not say anything

---

[27] Consult the author's article "A Messianic Perspective on Halloween."

[28] For a further examination of Paul's letter to the Galatians, consult the author's article "The Message of Galatians" and his commentary *Galatians for the Practical Messianic.*

about it[29]—and Colossians 2:16-17 is often turned on its head to actually judge those of us who keep them. These two verses often not read in light of the wider cotext of Colossians 2, and the actual problem present in Colossae that Paul is having to address.

A number of evangelical Christian commentators have rightfully concluded that the main error present in Colossae, that the Apostle Paul had to address, concerned a false philosophy (Colossians 2:8) that was some kind of Gnosticized-Jewish amalgamation of errors—a dangerous socio-religious soup of ideas unique to the Lycus Valley in Asia Minor.[30] While this was not necessarily the full blown Gnosticism of the Second and Third Centuries, there are enough clues in Colossians that it was a kind of proto-Gnosticism. This is seen by the usage of terms like *gnōsis* (γνῶσις), *plērōma* (πλήρωμα), and *sophia* (σοφία)—knowledge, fullness, and wisdom—directly used by Paul to subvert the errors of the false teachers (1:9-10, 26-28; 2:2-3; 3:10).[31] Their false philosophy involved some ascetic practices that involved worship of angels, and harsh treatment of the body (Colossians 2:18-21). The false philosophy advocated that Yeshua the Messiah was just one of various intermediaries between God the Father and humankind, and categorically denied that Yeshua was Divine (Colossians 2:9).

A typical Christian perspective of what Paul communicates in Colossians 2:16-17 is reflected in the *Ryrie Study Bible*, which remarks, "False teachers were evidently insisting on abstinence from certain foods and observance of certain days. These, Paul says, are shadows which have been dispersed by the coming of Christ."[32] Subsequently, today's Messianics who believe that by remembering the Sabbath, the appointed times, and eating kosher—we can learn things about the character of God—are thought by many to have looked backward in their faith and not forward to the Messiah. People like us are thus only able to grasp at shadows, and have lost the substance of the Lord.

---

[29] This is not to say that there are not Messianic people out there who harshly condemn Christians who do not observe *Shabbat*, the appointed times, or eat kosher. There are, and they have frequently brought a great deal of discredit to our faith community.

For a further examination of this, consult the relevant volumes of the *Messianic Helper Series* by Messianic Apologetics.

[30] D.A. Carson and Douglas J. Moo, *An Introduction to the New Testament*, second edition (Grand Rapids: Zondervan, 2005), pp 523-525; F.F. Bruce, *New International Commentary on the New Testament: The Epistles to the Colossians, to Philemon, and to the Ephesians* (Grand Rapids: Eerdmans, 1984), pp 17-26; Douglas J. Moo, *Pillar New Testament Commentary: The Letters to the Colossians and to Philemon* (Grand Rapids: Eerdmans, 2008), pp 46-60.

[31] For a summarization of Gnosticism, consult A.M. Renwick, "Gnosticism," in *ISBE*, 2:484-490.

[32] Charles C. Ryrie, ed., *Ryrie Study Bible*, NASB (Chicago: Moody Press, 1978), 1800.

The challenge, though, is in recognizing what things like the Sabbath or appointed times meant to the false teachers. How were these practices caught up in the false philosophy circulating in Colossae? Too frequently, Colossians 2:16-17 is just used as a sound byte, without any consideration for what the false philosophy actually was, and the other ascetic practices detailed (Colossians 2:18-21).

There were a wide variety of gross religious errors that had the real danger of affecting the Believers at Colossae. Before saying anything about the Biblical holidays or the Sabbath, Paul warns the Colossians, "See to it that no one takes you captive through philosophy and empty deception, according to the tradition of men, according to the elementary principles of the world, rather than according to Messiah" (Colossians 2:8). What would we define as "deceptive philosophy" (NIV) and "elemental spirits of the universe"[33] (RSV) here? What should we consider to be "according to human tradition"[34] (RSV)? Are the appointed times established by God in the Torah of human origin? Paul knew the Torah to be of Divine origin (Romans 7:7), and how it said "These are the appointed times of the LORD" (Leviticus 23:4). So, what the Colossians are warned against cannot be things established by God.

Ryrie correctly defines what is actually according to human origin as "the cosmic spirits of Hellenistic syncretism." He views that the Colossian false teaching was a "philosophy involved regulating their religious life by observing the movements of the stars, which they associated with the power of the angels who were worshipped by some."[35]

It is not very difficult to see that the philosophy and empty deception that Paul warned the Colossians about, are the base, humanistic, fallen religious beliefs of the world. This would first have pertained to the dominant religious system of Colossae and the Lycus Valley, that being standard Greco-Roman religion. This could have secondly pertained to any mystery religions or cults in the region. And thirdly, especially given the false philosophy's penchant for some kind of angel worship (Colossians 2:18), we can agree with Douglas J. Moo and how "The people combined this 'veneration of angels' with ascetic practices and rituals drawn from both paganism and Judaism, thereby creating a local syncretistic belief system that was being picked up and propagated by some Christians in Colossae."[36]

---

[33] Grk. *ta stoicheia tou kosmou* (τὰ στοιχεῖα τοῦ κόσμου); the same as appears in Galatians 4:3.

[34] Grk. *kata tēn paradosin tōn anthrōpōn* (κατὰ τὴν παράδοσιν τῶν ἀνθρώπων).

[35] Ryrie, 1800.

[36] Moo, *Colossians-Philemon*, 58.

The most damning feature of this false philosophy was, of course, its denigration of the Messiah Yeshua as just another intermediary. This is why immediately after warning the Colossians not to be led astray (Colossians 2:8), Paul must assert "For in Him all the fullness of Deity dwells in bodily form" (Colossians 2:9). This is a very powerful statement made by Paul, as the Greek word *theotēs* (θεότης) appears only once in the Apostolic Scriptures, in this verse, affirming Yeshua as God: "This word, meaning 'divinity,' occurs in the NT only in Col 2:9 (cf. 1:19-20). The one God, to whom all deity belongs, has given this fullness of deity to the incarnate Christ" (*TDNT*).[37] And Yeshua, being the *only* intermediary between God the Father and humanity to entreat for help **is made clear because of the significant saving work that He has accomplished for us!** Paul continues, writing,

"[A]nd in Him you have been made complete, and He is the head over all rule and authority; and in Him you were also circumcised with a circumcision made without hands, in the removal of the body of the flesh by the circumcision of Messiah; having been buried with Him in baptism, in which you were also raised up with Him through faith in the working of God, who raised Him from the dead. When you were dead in your transgressions and the uncircumcision of your flesh, He made you alive together with Him, having forgiven us all our transgressions" (Colossians 2:10-13).

These verses testify of the reality of how Yeshua's salvation provides a circumcision of the heart that is different from that of the flesh. The act of baptism or water immersion is symbolic of passing out of the world of death into new life in Him (Romans 6:3-4). While previously being dead in sin, Paul writes the Colossians that they have now found forgiveness via the work of the Messiah.

Paul further comments in Colossians 2:14 that Yeshua "canceled out the certificate of debt consisting of decrees against us, which was hostile to us; and He has taken it out of the way, having nailed it to the cross." While this passage is often interpreted as meaning that the Law of Moses was "nailed to the cross," this is not what the verse is saying. The Greek term *cheirographon* (χειρόγραφον) means "a **hand-written document, specif. a certificate of indebtedness, *account, record of* debts**" (*BDAG*).[38] Traditional views of Colossians 2:14 dating back to the Protestant Reformation often rightly associated the certificate of debt as either the record of human sin, or the guilt of human sin incurred before God.[39] Another common view of Colossians 2:14, similar to this,

---

[37] H. Kleinknecht, "*theótēs*," in Geoffrey W. Bromiley, ed., *Theological Dictionary of the New Testament*, abridged (Grand Rapids: Eerdmans, 1985), 330.

[38] *BDAG*, 1083.

[39] For one example, see John Wesley, *Explanatory Notes Upon the New Testament*, reprint (Peterborough, UK: Epworth Press, 2000), 747.

sees the certificate of debt as the pronouncement of condemnation that hung over Yeshua as He was dying on the cross (Matthew 27:37; Mark 15:26; Luke 23:38; John 19:19).

The primary issue handled in Colossians 2:14 is the condemnation that stood against people by sin, a record of debt that has now been paid for via the sacrifice of Yeshua. Yeshua took our sin upon Himself and His work provides atonement for our sin. *The condemnation pronounced by the Torah against sinners has been remitted*—a free gift of redemption available to all people. Following this, Paul then speaks of the final victory that the Messiah has over sin and against all principalities and powers:

"When He had disarmed the rulers and authorities, He made a public display of them, having triumphed over them through Him" (Colossians 2:15).

Any intermediary forces, such as the angels, that the Colossians were being tempted to either worship or entreat, were stripped of any authority they might have claimed over people by the Father resurrecting His Son, and Yeshua being supremely exalted to His right hand (cf. Philippians 2:9-11; Isaiah 45:21-23). It would have been entirely useless for any other intermediary to be sought, when it was Yeshua Himself who stood supreme over all principalities. In Paul's paralleling letter, he affirms,

"He brought [this] about in Messiah, when He raised Him from the dead and seated Him at His right hand in the heavenly *places*, far above all rule and authority and power and dominion, and every name that is named, not only in this age but also in the one to come" (Ephesians 1:20-21).

Sandwiched between Paul's assertion that Yeshua has triumphed supremely over the spiritual forces, and his remarks about the asceticism circulating in Colossae, is a short statement made about the Sabbath and appointed times:

"Therefore no one is to act as your judge in regard to food or drink or in respect to a festival or a new moon or a Sabbath day—things which are a *mere* shadow of what is to come; but the substance belongs to Messiah" (Colossians 2:16-17, NASU).

In what way were the Colossian Believers to whom Paul was writing not to take judgment? Were they not to allow themselves to be judged because they were not following these aspects of the Torah? Or, were they not to allow themselves to be judged because they did not consider the Sabbath or appointed times to have the same kind of value as the false teachers? If the latter is to be the accepted option, then not only would it concur with how the Jerusalem Council ruled in Acts 15 that the non-Jews coming to faith were anticipated to go to the local synagogue and learn from Moses' Teaching—but that **things like kosher eating, the appointed times, and the Sabbath were *mainline practices*** of the Colossian Believers living in accordance with God's Word. Various commentators have noted that when carefully read within its larger cotext, no condemnation of keeping the Sabbath or appointed times is intended, but rather how these things were taken up into the false philosophy—and the Colossians were not to feel judged because they viewed these things a little differently:

- Peter T. O'Brien: "For Israel the keeping of these holy days was evidence of obedience to God's law and a sign of her election among the nations. At Colossae, however, the sacred days were to be kept for the sake of the 'elemental spirits of the universe,' those astral powers who directed the course of the stars and relegated the order of the calendar. So Paul is not condemning the use of sacred days or seasons as such; it is the wrong motive involved when the observance of these days is bound up with the recognition of the elemental spirits."[40]

- Andrew T. Lincoln: "[T]here is no indication here that the motivation for abstinence from food and drink was due to observance of Torah....There is no hint that such special days are being observed because of the desire to obey Torah as such or because keeping them was a special mark of Jewish identity. Instead, it is probable that in the philosophy they were linked to a desire to please the cosmic powers."[41]

- Douglas J. Moo: "Only Sabbath observance that is connected inappropriately to a wider religious viewpoint is here being condemned. These interpreters [who agree] are quite right to emphasize the importance of interpreting contextually and historically. And they are also right, we have suggested, to argue that Sabbath was taken up into a larger, syncretistic mix."[42]

None of these commentators think that the Sabbath or appointed times are to be followed by Believers today, but they do recognize that we must read what is said in Colossians 2:16-17 in light of the larger issues being addressed. The Colossians were not to take any judgment for not adhering to the syncretistic false philosophy, which gave some sort of inappropriate significance to the Sabbath and appointed times. The Colossians were not to take judgment from these people, as they

---

[40] Peter T. O'Brien, *Word Biblical Commentary: Colossians, Philemon,* Vol. 44 (Nashville: Thomas Nelson, 1982), 139.

[41] Andrew T. Lincoln, "The Letter to the Colossians," in Leander E. Keck, ed., et. al., *New Interpreter's Bible,* Vol. 11 (Nashville: Abingdon, 2000), 139.

[42] Moo, *Colossians-Philemon,* 221.

would be looked down upon by the false teachers for somehow not being "enlightened" from their false philosophy (cf. Colossians 2:19). Inappropriate observance of the Sabbath and appointed times was the issue.

The false philosophy circulating in Colossae was taking people away from Yeshua the Messiah, and so Paul makes the point to remind his readers that the true meaning of things like the Sabbath and appointed times is found in Him: "These are a shadow of the things to come, but the substance belongs to Christ" (Colossians 2:17, ESV). Yet as you have probably noticed, a relatively literal version like the NASU renders v. 17 by saying that the Biblical appointments were but "a *mere* shadow of what is to come." Does this not imply that they are no longer important? Can things like the Sabbath or appointed times no longer inform God's people about His plan of salvation history, and the Second Coming of the Messiah?

It is notable that the New American Standard translators took a liberty and placed the word "*mere*" in italics, meaning that the word was not originally in the Greek text. The important clause reads *ha estin skia tōn mellontōn* (ἅ ἐστιν σκιὰ τῶν μελλόντων).[43] The placement of "*mere*" in the English text is not implied by the context of the sentence, unlike an understood verb or article that was not written by the original author and could legitimately be written in italics.[44] This is unseen in the Revised Standard Version rendering, which does not use italics: "These are only a shadow of what is to come..."

Even more important to be aware of is how the New International Version renders v. 17 with a past tense verb: "These are a shadow of the things that were to come..." The NIV might not add "*mere*" or "only," but the present tense participle *mellontōn* (μελλόντων) means "things coming,"[45] not "things that were to come." The argument presented for rendering a present tense verb as a past tense verb, is that Torah practices like the Sabbath and appointed times have reached their conclusion, and have nothing more to teach God's people.

In O'Brien's estimation, "The expression 'things to come'...does not refer to what lies in the future from the standpoint of the writer...so pointing, for example, to the time of the Second Coming."[46] The reason he gives, that *mellontōn* has to be translated in the past tense, is that

---

[43] The Greek word *monos* (μόνος), which can appear "as adverb, *alone, only, merely*" (Joseph H. Thayer, *Thayer's Greek-English Lexicon of the New Testament* [Peabody, MA: Hendrickson, 2003], 418), rendered as "mere" in Mark 6:8 in the NASU, does not appear in the Greek source text of Colossians 2:17.

[44] Other unimplied usages of "mere" in the NASU, where *monos* does not occur in the source text, appear in: 1 Corinthians 3:3, 4; 1 Timothy 1:4; Hebrews 9:24.

[45] Cleon L. Rogers, Jr. and Cleon L. Rogers III, *The New Linguistic and Exegetical Key to the Greek New Testament* (Grand Rapids: Zondervan, 1998), 465.

[46] O'Brien, *Colossians-Philemon*, 140.

"then the σκιά ('shadow') would not have been superseded and the ordinances referred to would retain their importance."[47] O'Brien's words are actually quite telling here: **if there are still things to come, then Shabbat, the appointed times, and even the dietary laws have lessons to teach God's people today.** And this is exactly why today's Messianic Believers remember them! There is no legitimate justification to misrepresent a verb tense to fit one's theological presupposition as has been done here.

Colossians 2:17 raises an important question for us, because this text also says, regarding the Biblical appointments, that "the substance belongs to Messiah." Rendered literally, *to de sōma tou Christou* (τὸ δὲ σῶμα τοῦ Χριστοῦ) is "and the body *is* of the Christ" (YLT). This is reflected in the CJB rendering of "but the body is of the Messiah." There is debate as to what the proper context of the word *sōma* (σῶμα) relates to in this verse. Some interpret it as meaning that while no outside person is to judge Believers in matters of eating, drinking, a Sabbath day, or festival, it is only the Body of Messiah that is able to judge. Others, however, interpret the word *sōma* in relation to the things that are coming, and that the "substance" (RSV, NASU) or "reality" (NIV) of the appointed times is found in Yeshua.

Sōma has a variety of meanings, including *"body, living body, physical body; the body* (of Christ), *the church; dead body, corpse; the reality or substance* (as opposed to a shadow)" (CGEDNT).[48] Is Paul comparing *sōma* to "body," i.e., the Body of Messiah judging in regard to the appointed times? Or, is he comparing *sōma* to *skia* (σκιά) or "shadow," meaning that the appointed times are a shadow, and the true substance or meaning of them, is found in Yeshua?

Given the tenor of the false philosophy circulating in Colossae, which denigrated the Divinity of Yeshua, His atoning work, and which sought intercession via other spiritual intermediaries—*sōma* as "substance" is to be preferred. The most that things like the Sabbath or appointed times could mean for the false teachers would be an incomplete shadow, because they had missed the whole point of why God gave them to His people. While *sōma* (σῶμα) can mean "body" as in the Body of Messiah, with *sōma* contrasted to *skia*, it has to mean "**substantive reality,** *the thing itself, the reality* in imagery of a body that casts a shadow, in contrast to σκιά [*skia*]" (BDAG).[49] The issue is, as properly extrapolated by the New English Bible, "the solid reality is Christ's."

---

[47] Ibid.

[48] Barclay M. Newman, Jr., *A Concise Greek-English Dictionary of the New Testament* (Stuttgart: United Bible Societies/Deutche Bibelgesellschaft, 1971), 177.

[49] BDAG, 984.

Contrary to recognizing the true reality or substance of the Sabbath and appointed times as being Yeshua the Messiah, the false teachers sought spiritual help and enlightenment from other sources. Paul warned the Colossians, "Let no one keep defrauding you of your prize by delighting in self-abasement and the worship of the angels, taking his stand on *visions* he has seen, inflated without cause by his fleshly mind" (Colossians 2:18). Whether one takes "worship of angels" (Grk. *thrēskeia tōn angelōn*, θρησκείᾳ τῶν ἀγγέλων) to be worship directed to angels, or an ascetic attempt to join into the worship of angels in Heaven—the point is made that practices from God like the Sabbath or appointed times were being abused. They were caught up in a philosophy of "false humility" (NIV) that likely inflicted some physical harm on adherents via intense fasting,[50] in an effort to induce visions and pierce the inter-dimensional veil that was off limits for humans. And the most that adherents would be able to find, according to Paul, would be shadows.

But is there a proper way to honor things like the Sabbath and appointed times? Surely if the Apostle Paul only criticized their improper observance as part of the Colossian false philosophy, then there can be a proper way to remember these things—as their shadow or outline points us to the substance—and helps us to understand not only "what is to come," but also *better understand* what has already come. The work of Yeshua does not eliminate or disperse the shadow, but rather shows the greater reality that the shadow prefigures or outlines. In making the Sabbath and appointed times a part of our weekly and yearly faith experience, *we can learn more about the Lord we love and serve*.

If we are convicted that the appointed times are still to be followed today, then as Messianic Believers we have to understand that the true meaning or substance of them is found in the Messiah. We honor the Lord by observing His appointed times, and by remembering what Yeshua has done for us. The true significance of the seventh-day Sabbath, the appointed times, and indeed all of the Torah's practices are found in Messiah Yeshua, and the example that He lived for us. As Roger Bullard validly remarks, "Dietary laws and calendrical observances point beyond themselves to Christ, the reality."[51] The Biblical holidays explain the pattern of the Messiah's life, His Second Coming, and the themes of eternity. When we as Messianic Believers gather to remember them, we gather to not only remember the events they commemorate in the Torah, but also what they represent to us who believe in Yeshua. We do not just observe the Torah for the sake of

---

[50] Rendered as "self-abasement" in the NASU, *tapeinophrosunē* (ταπεινοφροσύνη) is often related to fasting (*BDAG*, 989).

[51] Roger Bullard, "The Letter of Paul to the Colossians," in Walter J. Harrelson, ed., et. al., *New Interpreter's Study Bible*, NRSV (Nashville: Abingdon, 2003), 2111.

observing the Torah. We are to keep these things because they point to Yeshua, and speak volumes to us about who He is, what He has done, and what He will do for us.

The importance of keeping the Lord's appointments for Believers cannot be overstated because when speaking of the Exodus and events in the wilderness, the Apostle Paul wrote, "Now these things happened to them as an example, and they were written for our instruction, upon whom the ends of the ages have come" (1 Corinthians 10:11). The RSV actually says that "these things happened to them as a warning." If we find ourselves being the last generation "upon whom the ends of the ages have come," or we at least are nearing that last generation—how are we expected to understand God's redemptive plan for humanity and the end-times if we do not learn about the appointed times He has specified for us? How are we supposed to properly understand what is to befall Planet Earth?

If we do not keep the appointed times as God has told us, are we libel to misunderstand His prophetic plan for the ages? The "fixed times" (Leviticus 23:3, NJPS) of the Lord tell us when He plans to meet with us, especially regarding the Messiah's Second Coming. By keeping the appointed times and knowing their significance, can concepts such as the any-moment, random pre-tribulation rapture be theologically supported? Or, will we understand that there is a definitive pattern in the set seasons of the God of Israel, that we can only fully understand by keeping, as opposed to just studying, the *moedim*?[52]

Evangelical Believers have swelled the Messianic movement in the past two decades (1990s-2000s) precisely because they have taken hold of the important lessons and spiritual significance in things like the Sabbath, Biblical holidays, and kosher eating. They have seen the substance of Yeshua in the weekly day of rest, the Passover *seder*, the giving of the Law and outpouring of the Spirit at *Shavuot*, the blowing of the *shofar* and future resurrection on *Yom Teruah/Rosh HaShanah*, tabernacling with the Lord at *Sukkot*, and even (although it is extra-Biblical) lighting the *menorah* at *Chanukah*. In eating kosher they have learned how God wishes us to separate holy and unholy things, even in our diet, and how it can benefit our health. These Messianic Believers have not embraced these important aspects of God's Torah to appease the elemental spirits (Colossians 2:8) or worship angels (Colossians 2:18), **but to do things that Jesus did.**

---

[52] Note that while there are many Christian books written on the prophetic significance of the appointed times, almost all of them are written by those *who do not keep them* as a standard element of their praxis of faith. Should we accept prophetic interpretations related to the *moedim* by those who do not keep them, and hence do not understand them as fully as one who does keep them?

In our remembrance of the appointed times, we do need to heed Paul's words to the Colossians, and not find ourselves remembering these things with any kind of ascetic ideas in mind. We keep the Sabbath and appointed times to obey the Lord, and to be instructed on how they depict His plan for the ages. If we can remember these things properly, then our faith community can influence others as to how important they are. Unfortunately, many Christians are unable to read Colossians 2:16-17 in light of the dominant issues circulating in Ancient Colossae, and they think that in learning to appreciate the shadow, Messianic Believers have completely forgotten the substance. Contrary to this though, if we are obedient via the love we have for God and for one another, then we can properly understand the role that the *shadow* plays in us recognizing the *substance*—our Messiah Yeshua![53]

Romans 14:5-6

"One person regards one day above another, another regards every day alike. Each person must be fully convinced in his own mind. He who observes the day, observes it for the Lord, and he who eats, does so for the Lord, for he gives thanks to God; and he who eats not, for the Lord he does not eat, and gives thanks to God."

Many of today's Christian laypersons, reading Romans 14, think that they automatically know what the circumstances being addressed are: the Apostle Paul does not consider matters of sacred days or eating to be that important any more. Romans 14:5-6 are quoted to Messianic Believers as an indication that not only are the days one celebrates as holy inconsequential to God, but so is what one eats likewise inconsequential. Messianic Believers can choose to keep *Shabbat* and the appointed times, and eat kosher, if they want to—but it is thought that these are no longer definite requirements for His people. These are now only matters of conscience that are to be left up to individual choice. Unfortunately, though, rather than letting Messianic Believers keep *Shabbat*, the appointed times, and a kosher diet without any interference or harassment, Romans 14:5-6 are verses often used to unfairly judge those of us who keep them—quite contrary to the tenor of what(ever) Paul says.

The *NIV Study Bible* reflects the most common evangelical Christian point of view of what Romans 16:5-6 says, stating, "Some feel that this refers primarily to the Sabbath, but it is probably a reference to all the special days of the OT ceremonial law...The importance of personal conviction in disputable matters of conduct runs through this

---

[53] For a further examination of Paul's letter to the Colossians, consult the author's article "The Message of Colossians and Philemon" and his commentary *Colossians and Philemon for the Practical Messianic*.

passage."[54] From this vantage point, the days a person regards as sacred should be open for interpretation and application. Church tradition has determined that Sunday is an acceptable "Sabbath," and that Christmas and Easter are acceptable holidays to celebrate in place of the Torah-prescribed holidays. If a person wants to follow the Old Testament in this regard, and not the traditions of today's Church, he or she is not to be looked down upon, but neither is it to be mandated in any way. It is all a matter of one's personal value judgments.

If one follows this conclusion to its logical end, however, then observing modern Christian holidays like Christmas and Easter are also totally a matter of conscience, and people can choose to opt out of them if they want, not being mandated in Scripture. They do not have to go to Church on Sunday. Tuesday could be an acceptable Sabbath, independent of either the seventh or first days of the week, and if someone wanted to, Christmas could be celebrated on the Fourth of July, as opposed to December 25. Dates or seasons when religious events are commemorated do not matter, as it is all an issue of choice, as opposed to God's prescription. Yet it is safe to surmise that many Christians would not want to celebrate Christmas in the middle of the July Summer, much less consider holidays established by Church tradition to be "optional." They would surely frown on people who do not go to Church on Sunday, choosing to dismiss assembling together as unimportant (cf. Hebrews 10:25).

Romans 14 is one of the most ambiguous chapters of Scripture for not only today's Messianic Bible teachers, who largely ignore it, but also some of today's Christian commentators. Everyone can easily agree upon a cursory reading of Romans 14:1-16 that some kind of issue regarding special days and eating is being addressed—but what those things specifically were, and how they divided the Believers in Rome, is something else. It is rightfully agreed that the Apostle Paul was warning the Roman Believers—a mixed group of Jewish and non-Jewish Believers—to not be divided over minor scruples, *but that might be about all we know for sure.* Romans 14:13 issues the instructive word, "Therefore let us not judge one another anymore, but rather determine this—not to put an obstacle or a stumbling block in a brother's way."

What these things actually involved for the Roman Believers may require a closer reading of Paul's admonishment than is commonly seen by many who encounter Romans—precisely because "opinions" (Romans 14:1) are being addressed. These opinions may concern the Law of Moses, but not as directly as some may think. C.E.B. Cranfield issues a bit of caution in his Romans commentary, "Some recent commentators have exhibited great confidence in their approach to the

---

[54] Kenneth L. Barker, ed., et. al., *NIV Study Bible* (Grand Rapids: Zondervan, 2002), 1768.

interpretation of this section. This we find surprising; for it seems to us to be extremely difficult to decide with certainty what exactly the problem is with which Paul is concerned in this section."[55] Our examination of Romans 14:5-6 cannot be divorced from the larger cotext, and most especially the larger themes seen in Paul's letter. And, it might be a bit hasty to automatically conclude that the Sabbath, appointed times, and dietary laws are being specifically considered— because they are commandments laid forth in God's Torah, and not "opinions" held by human individuals.

One of the main overarching themes of the Epistle to the Romans is not only for Paul to "promote" his theology and gospel presentation— as he is planning to use Rome as a hub for ministry outreach to Spain (Romans 15:24) and will need the Roman Believers' support—but for him also to express the necessity for the Jewish and non-Jewish Believers in Rome to all be united. This was in no small part complicated by the Jewish expulsion from Rome by Claudius in 49 C.E. (cf. Acts 18:2), and how the Jewish Believers were now returning to fellowships where they were no longer the dominant group of people and/or the leaders. The clash of cultures created by significant numbers of Greeks and Romans now coming to faith, caused many of them to look down on the Jewish people, who were largely not answering to the gospel as much as the nations at large were. Paul wants to assure these non-Jews that they are dependent on the salvific root of Judaism (Romans 11:17-18), and that they *rely more* on the Jews than the Jews rely on them. Paul is absolutely concerned about the unity that is required within the *ekklēsia*, and so he takes it upon himself to discuss issues that divided the Believers in Rome, and/or their sub-assemblies.

One of the main issues that could have been very divisive would have been what to eat at the various fellowship meals, as eating is the main issue addressed in Romans 14:1-16. Was the Apostolic decree being followed, should meat be served (Acts 15:20), which required a degree of kosher to be respected? Did the meat being served have its blood properly removed? Where did the meat come from: a Jewish slaughterhouse or the Roman marketplace? Even if the blood were removed from the meat, some Jewish Believers could have been highly cautious about where the meat was purchased, if the Jewish meat sources were not selling to the Believers.[56] Some Jewish Believers could have easily frowned on any meat from the Roman market, even if it

---

[55] C.E.B. Cranfield, *International Critical Commentary: Romans 9-16* (London: T&T Clark, 1979), 690.

[56] Consult Ben Witherington III, *Paul's Letter to the Romans: A Socio-Historical Commentary* (Grand Rapids: Eerdmans, 2004), pp 334-345, for a summary of the different options.

were acceptable according to Biblical law, and was specially butchered for clients who were Believers.

Paul begins this vignette by contrasting the eating of meat versus only eating vegetables. He states, "Now accept the one who is weak in faith, *but* not for *the purpose of* passing judgment on his opinions. One person has faith that he may eat all things, but he who is weak eats vegetables *only*" (Romans 14:1-2). The issue as first seen here is not that of following the *kashrut* laws of clean and unclean, but rather of eating just vegetables and/or eating meat. The Torah does not require a person to be a vegetarian, even if there are some restrictions placed on eating meat. Yet those who have the faith to eat all, meat and vegetables, are not to pass judgment upon those who follow a vegetarian diet out of conviction. Philip F. Esler confirms how the scene depicted, is what was being served during Roman fellowship meals:

"Paul seemed to be responding to dysfunctional gatherings of the Christ-movement in Rome rather than the total isolation of one group from another. Perhaps we should imagine gatherings in a strong person's house where there is a meal with meat and vegetables, but the weak will only eat the vegetables and are abused by the strong for doing so."[57]

The one interesting clue that Paul gives about what is being eaten is, "All things indeed are clean" (Romans 14:20), the Greek term *katharos* (καθαρός) having been employed in the Septuagint to describe those animals considered ritually clean and acceptable for eating (Heb. *tahor*, טָהוֹר).[58] Seeing this, it would be most unlikely that the meat served at the fellowship meals fell outside the guidelines of clean and unclean animals of Leviticus 11 and Deuteronomy 14. But how acceptable would the meat be for some Jewish Believers—with clean meat possibly having to come from Roman sources?

The high point of this instruction is clear: Paul does not want brethren to judge one another (Romans 14:13), as it is a relatively minor issue in comparison to other aspects of faith. But is Paul really discussing the continued validity of the Sabbath, appointed times, and kosher dietary laws, now no longer being necessary for Believers in Yeshua—or is he talking about something else? Many think that the validity of *kashrut* is the issue, because later Paul will describe how "I know and am convinced in the Lord Yeshua that nothing is unclean in itself; but to him who thinks anything to be unclean, to him it is unclean" (Romans 14:14). Yet there is a significant translation issue with this verse, because the flesh of animals that is declared "unclean" in the Torah is not in view.

---

[57] Philip F. Esler, *Conflict and Identity in Romans: The Social Setting of Paul's Letter* (Minneapolis: Augsberg Fortress, 2003), 350.

[58] Genesis 7:2-3, 8; 8:20; Leviticus 4:12; 6:11; 7:19; Ezra 6:20; cf. Moo, *Romans*, 860 fn#63.

Almost all Bible versions read with "unclean" in Romans 14:14. The Hebrew word rendered as "unclean" in the food lists of Leviticus 11 and Deuteronomy 14 is *tamei* (טָמֵא), employed in direct relation to "ceremonially unclean animals" (*HALOT*).[59] In the LXX, *tamei* was rendered by the Greek word *akathartos* (ἀκάθαρτος), "*impure,* *unclean*," specifically "of foods" (*BDAG*).[60] *Akathartos* does not appear in Romans 14:14, and the rendering of "unclean" is inaccurate. The Greek word that appears instead is *koinos* (κοινός), "This word means 'common'...in the sense of common ownership, property, ideas, etc" (*TDNT*).[61] *Koinos* relates "**to being of little value because of being common, common, ordinary, profane,**" and can concern "that which ordinary people eat, in contrast to those of more refined tastes" (*BDAG*).[62]

Koinos is employed in the Apocrypha where "swine and unclean animals" (1 Maccabees 1:47) were sacrificed in the Temple precincts. Yet these *ktēnē koina* (κτήνη κοινὰ), in addition to the swine, were likely Biblically clean animals sacrificed by the Seleucid Greeks, but not at all being *tamim* (תָּמִים) or fit for sacrifice in God's holy place.[63] Although being pagans they did sacrifice pigs, traditional Greco-Roman religion did use Biblically clean, albeit common, animals in their sacrifices as well. Similarly, a Greco-Roman diet would have involved the eating of cattle, sheep, goats, and various fowl, which are listed as "clean" on the food lists of the Torah.

The LITV renders *koinos* properly with "common," noting the careful nuances communicated in Paul's instruction to the Roman Believers:

"I know and am persuaded in the Lord Jesus that nothing by itself is common; except to the one deeming anything to be common, it is common" (Romans 14:14, LITV).

"Common food," possibly served at some of the fellowship meals, would not be the same as "unclean 'food'" (which itself is an oxymoron as God does not consider "unclean food" *to be food*). "Common food" would include those things that are Biblically clean, but perhaps were considered inedible by a highly conservative sector of Jewish Believers in Rome.[64] Paul instructs the "strong" Roman Believers that they are not to put any of the "weak" Roman Believers down for abstaining from such meat at fellowship gatherings. We can safely assume, especially

---

[59] Ludwig Koehler and Walter Baumgartner, eds., *The Hebrew & Aramaic Lexicon of the Old Testament*, 2 vols. (Leiden, the Netherlands: Brill, 2001), 1:376.

[60] *BDAG*, 34.

[61] F. Hauck, "*koinós*," in *TDNT*, 447.

[62] *BDAG*, 552.

[63] I.e., Exodus 12:5; Leviticus 1:3, 10; 3:1, 6, 9, etc.

[64] Such "common food" today would be Biblically clean meats, but meats that would probably not have a Rabbinical stamp of approval on them.

given the orientation of meat as prescribed by the Apostolic decree, that the meat was that of Biblically-clean animals, yet something has arisen because certain people are not going to eat the meat. If the meat were butchered properly with the blood removed, but if it came from a Roman meat source, the "weak" could have chosen not to eat it. Paul instructs how *they are not to be looked down upon*, because they hold to such a conviction.

Paul's discussion here concerns "disputable matters" (Romans 14:1, NIV). Unless we are prepared to discount Paul's previous word about Believers upholding God's Torah in Messiah (Romans 3:31), this would involve issues for which there was no definite Biblical solution, unlike the flesh of animals that was definitively declared "unclean" in the Torah (*tamei/akathartos*). Noting that opinions or disputable matters is the issue (Romans 14:1),[65] Stern comments, "Where Scripture gives a clear word, personal opinion must give way. But where the Word of God is subject to various possible interpretations, let each be persuaded in his own mind."[66] Romans 14 discusses such *halachic* opinions between conservative Jewish Believers and the more moderate non-Jewish Believers. Hegg further concludes,

"This in itself should...put to rest the notion that Paul is discussing issues of Sabbath and kosher food laws, for though in our times these might be considered matters of 'opinion,' they surely could not have been so construed in Paul's day. What must fall under the category of 'opinions' are those things for which both sides could equally be considered righteous and worthy."[67]

What a person eats—especially at fellowship meals—is ultimately not as important as being united in the love and hope of the gospel. *We are to be identified as changed people by the work of the Lord within us.* In this light, eating is a relatively minor matter, **even if all of the food available to be eaten is clean or "kosher,"** because there are other things that are far more important in the Kingdom of God. Paul says, "the kingdom of God is not eating and drinking, but righteousness and peace and joy in the Holy Spirit" (Romans 14:17). "Drinking" is also added to the mix here, and it is notable that we consider how the Torah includes no general prohibition on consuming alcohol as a part of normal life. Many, however, could easily have held to the opinion that drinking alcohol was not for them.

Paul himself would have had no problem eating any of the "common" food served at the Roman fellowship meals, but he strongly

---

[65] Grk. *dialogismos* (διαλογισμός); "content of reasoning or conclusion reached through use of reason, *thought, opinion, reasoning, design*" (BDAG, 232).
[66] Stern, *Jewish New Testament Commentary*, pp 434-435.
[67] Tim Hegg, *Paul's Epistle to the Romans, Volume 2: Chapters 9-16* (Tacoma, WA: TorahResource, 2007), 408.

warned against those who considered themselves "strong," who looked down upon the "weak," who would not eat their meat out of personal conviction. Such unnecessary judgment could only cause problems for the *ekklēsia*.

Within this discussion of eating (Romans 14:1-2 and 14:17), as Moo indicates, "Paul interrupts his theological argument to cite another point,"[68] and so he discusses the secondary issue of sacred days, to show the supposed "strong" why they should not be looking down upon those they considered "weak." But does his discussion about eating meat get interrupted with the statements about sacred days in v. 3 or v. 4, or even v. 5? Paul's instruction simply details how there is to be no judgment taking place between the Believers in Rome:

"The one who eats is not to regard with contempt the one who does not eat, and the one who does not eat is not to judge the one who eats, for God has accepted him. Who are you to judge the servant of another? To his own master he stands or falls; and he will stand, for the Lord is able to make him stand" (Romans 14:3-4).

The issue that I would like to raise is whether vs. 3-4 are a continuation of the remarks made in vs. 1-2, or if they help to introduce the statements about sacred days in vs. 5-6. V. 3 employs the participles *esthiōn* (ἐσθίων) and *mē esthiōn* (μὴ ἐσθίων), referring to the "eater" and "non-eater." Is this referring to a person who eats all, and one who does not eat all at the fellowship meals—or a person who eats, versus one who does not eat or fasts? Does this relate to the actions described in vs. 1-2 preceding about meals involving meat and vegetables, or the actions following in vs. 5-6 about sacred days and eating/not eating?

Paul wants the non-Jewish Believers in Rome to be very sensitive to some distinct Jewish needs. Vs. 1-2 lay out the general principle of not looking down on those who do not eat everything at the fellowship meals. Vs. 3-4, however, raise the stakes on looking down on some of the sensitivities of these Jewish Believers. These are people who are convicted in their hearts that what they are doing is right before the Lord. While both are to respect the others' opinion, Paul specifically wants the non-Jewish Believers to know, "Who are you to judge someone else's servant? To his own master he stands or falls. And he will stand, for the Lord is able to make him stand" (Romans 14:4, NIV). All are certainly servants of the Lord, but *only to the Lord* are individuals ultimately accountable for their opinions—not flawed human beings.

Asserting that both the "weak" and "strong" will answer to the same God for their convictions or opinions, Paul issues his instruction about sacred days:

"One person regards one day above another, another regards every day *alike*. Each person must be fully convinced in his own mind. He

---

[68] Moo, *Romans*, 841.

who observes the day, observes it for the Lord, and he who eats, does so for the Lord, for he gives thanks to God; and he who eats not, for the Lord he does not eat, and gives thanks to God" (Romans 14:5-6).

The Lord is honored by those who consider certain days special, and those who consider all days alike. The eater (*esthiōn*) thanks Him, and the non-eater (*mē esthiōn*) thanks Him.[69] So, a majority of commentators extrapolate this and conclude that the Sabbath, appointed times, and dietary laws are now, at most, just a matter of choice (for Jewish Believers in Yeshua).[70] It is asserted that God accepts those who keep these Torah rituals, but He also accepts those who do not. We should probably pause here for a moment and take a look at two commentators who hold to this view, should any evangelical Christian reading this have ever looked down upon a Messianic Jew or a Messianic non-Jew, who is convicted of the Lord that these practices are indeed for today:

- Douglas J. Moo: "The believer who sets aside certain days...or who observes the Sabbath, does so because he or she sincerely believes this honors the Lord. Similarly, both the believer who eats anything without discrimination and the believer who refuses to eat certain things 'gives thanks' to God at their mealtimes and are motivated in their respective practices by a desire to glorify the Lord."[71]

- Ben Witherington III: "The attitude expressed here is much like that expressed by John Wesley and others: in essentials unity, in non-essentials one thinks and lets think, all in all things charity and love. While Paul believes in persuasion and in imperatives, he also believes in allowing people the freedom to make up their minds on a host of things, so long as it is within the realm of what could reasonably be said to be in accord with the will of God..."[72]

While neither one of these theologians thinks that keeping the seventh-day Sabbath or dietary laws is necessary for today—I do not think that they would look down with resentment or harsh judgment toward those who do. They would consider it an issue of personal choice and preference, and hopefully wish Messianics the best in their

---

[69] Note how the NIV adds "meat" to v. 6: "He who eats meat, eats to the Lord." However, *kreas* (κρέας) only appears later in v. 21.

[70] F.F. Bruce, *Tyndale New Testament Commentaries: Romans* (Grand Rapids: Eerdmans, 1985), pp 231-232; James D.G. Dunn, *Word Biblical Commentary: Romans 9-16*, Vol 38b (Dallas: Word Books, 1988), pp 804-807; Moo, *Romans*, pp 841-843.

[71] Moo, *Romans*, 843.

[72] Witherington, *Romans*, 336.

trying to honor the Lord. This does not mean that there are not Christians who look down with disdain at Messianics, because there are. And, much of this is reciprocated with some disdain toward Christians on the Messianic end, which is equally wrong and reprehensible, and needs to be remedied by Messianics who encourage their fellow Believers to change via a positive testimony.

The challenge we have to consider is what Romans 14:5-6 meant to the Romans. While it is easy to just jump ahead and automatically conclude that the Sabbath, appointed times, and kosher are being discussed—this may be a little too convenient. While a Jewish orientation of things being eaten and sacred days is certain, it concerns matters of disputable *halachah*. N.T. Wright, one of today's leading Pauline scholars, points out how "It is interesting...that he does not refer to the sabbath explicitly."[73] Moo also has to indicate how "Whether the specific point at issue was the observance of the great Jewish festivals, regular days of fasting, or the Sabbath is difficult to say."[74] Indeed, there is no mention at all of the word "Sabbath" (Grk. *sabbaton*, σάββατον) in the Epistle to the Romans, much less in ch. 14! James R. Edwards makes a valid observation, stating, "Paul leaves *day* undefined, perhaps out of deference to the arguing parties. It may refer to Jewish fast days (Monday, Thursday)."[75]

Are the days that some Jewish Believers might regard as being a bit "more sacred than another" (Romans 14:5, NIV) some kind of fast days? Both observing special days and eating or not eating, are tied together, which means that fast days are definitely within the window of possibilities. V. 6 compares and contrasts the eater (*esthiōn*) and the non-eater (*mē esthiōn*), which could easily be viewed as one who eats on a day considered very special to some people, where those people do not eat, or fast:

"The one minding the day, he minds it to the Lord. And the one not minding the day, he does not mind it to the Lord. The one eating, he eats to the Lord; for he gives thanks to God. And the one not eating, he does not eat to the Lord, and gives thanks to God" (Romans 14:6, LITV).

---

[73] N.T. Wright, "The Letter to the Romans," in Leander E. Keck, ed. et. al., *New Interpreter's Bible* (Nashville: Abingdon, 2002), 10:736.

[74] Moo, *Romans*, 842.
He does, however, conclude "we would expect that the Sabbath, at least, would be involved."

[75] James R. Edwards, "Romans," in *New Interpreter's Study Bible*, 2030.
John Reumann similarly notes how this could be "the sabbath or holy days for fasting or feasting" ("Romans," in James D.G. Dunn and John W. Rogerson, eds., *Eerdmans Commentary on the Bible* [Grand Rapids: Eerdmans, 2003], 1308), indicating the range of possibilities in the sacred days mentioned.

Hegg summarizes how "Paul...kept the Sabbath (Acts 17:2) and walked strictly according to the Torah (Acts 21:24)....[I]t is unthinkable that with such a passing statement Paul could abolish a Torah commandment that was one of the central issues in his day. And all without even the slightest hint or backlash! If Paul had taught that the Sabbath was no longer viable, this would have been added to the offenses his opponents listed against him..."[76]

So indeed, if some kind of optional fast days are the issue in Romans 14:5-6, as both Hegg[77] and I conclude, they would have been some serious opinions and convictions for which any non-Jewish Believer in Rome would have needed to be highly sensitive to his or her fellow Jewish Believers. When considering what they could have included, these fast days **would have been far more serious to consider** than the vegetables and/or meat served at fellowship meals.

The only Biblical time God's people are explicitly commanded to fast is on *Yom Kippur*. Leviticus 23:27 specifies, "On exactly the tenth day of this seventh month is the day of atonement; it shall be a holy convocation for you, and you shall humble your souls." It is clearly identified in Acts 27:9 as "the fast." However, other than references in the Scriptures to *Yom Kippur*, there is not very much more that the Bible has to say about fasting—even though fasting can be a very beneficial spiritual procedure. Fasting on certain days are often times when each individual must be convinced in his or her own mind. Fasting is often a matter solely of individual choice and spiritual conviction, from which one can clearly benefit.

The tradition of "Monday and Thursday are set aside for public fasts" (t. *Ta'anit* 2:4)[78] was established in Second Temple Judaism, because fasting was largely prohibited for the Sabbath and festivals (b.*Eruvin* 41a). The more likely, more serious days of fasting to be considered, though, were some fixed fast days established by the Jews who returned from the Babylonian exile, established to remember important events in Jewish history. Jacob Milgrom summarizes,

"Fixed fast days are first mentioned by the post-Exilic prophet Zechariah who proclaims the word of the Lord thus: 'The fast of the fourth month, the fast of the fifth, the fast of the seventh and the fast of the tenth...' (Zech. 8:19; cf. 7:3, 5). Jewish tradition has it that these fasts commemorate the critical events which culminated in the destruction of the Temple: the tenth of Tevet (the tenth month), the beginning of the siege of Jerusalem; the 17th of Tammuz (the fourth month), the breaching of the walls; the ninth of Av (the fifth month), when the

---

[76] Tim Hegg, *It is Often Said*, 2 vols. (Littleton, CO: First Fruits of Zion, 2003), 1:18.

[77] Hegg, *Romans Vol. 2*, pp 416-417.

[78] Jacob Neusner, ed., *The Tosefta: Translated from the Hebrew With a New Introduction*, 2 vols. (Peabody, MA: Hendrickson, 2002), 1:625.

Temple was destroyed; and the third of Tishri (the seventh month), when Gedaliah, the Babylonian-appointed governor of Judah, was assassinated" (*EJ*).[79]

If these are the days remembered by the one who does not eat in Romans 14:6, then the sensitivity that the "strong" would have to demonstrate toward the "weak" is definitely intensified. Keeping these fasts would be something that was entirely optional as far as one's faith practice was concerned. Yet remembering the siege of Jerusalem and the destruction of the Temple, by fasting and entreating the Lord for such events never to happen again, are worthy things to reflect upon—still largely observed in Judaism today. They may not be required, per se, but no mature Believer would ever in his or her right mind look with disdain upon others who are convicted that these times are worthy moments to abstain from food and pray before God. *They are high convictions deserving of respect.*

Viewing the sacred days of Romans 14:5-6 as fast days observed by many of the Jewish Believers in Rome, the Apostle Paul was very clear on how these things are done as unto the Lord. His instruction is quite clear to those who would look down with any disdain on those who would treat these times as being serious:

"For not one of us lives for himself, and not one dies for himself; for if we live, we live for the Lord, or if we die, we die for the Lord; therefore whether we live or die, we are the Lord's. For to this end Messiah died and lived again, that He might be Lord both of the dead and of the living. But you, why do you judge your brother? Or you again, why do you regard your brother with contempt? For we will all stand before the judgment seat of God. For it is written, 'AS I LIVE, SAYS THE LORD, EVERY KNEE SHALL BOW TO ME, AND EVERY TONGUE SHALL GIVE PRAISE TO GOD' [Isaiah 45:23]. So then each one of us will give an account of himself to God. Therefore let us not judge one another anymore, but rather determine this—not to put an obstacle or a stumbling block in a brother's way" (Romans 14:7-13).

Paul is much more serious about the issue of those who observe certain days as sacred, not choosing to eat on them—then over what the Roman Believers eat or do not eat at their fellowship meals, mentioning how we both live and die for the Lord. Many of the Jewish Believers in Rome would have considered fast days like the Ninth of Av, for example, to be very important times of spiritual intercession and prayer, so that great catastrophe never befell the Jewish people again. The non-Jewish Believers, perhaps not having that close a connection to the Temple in Jerusalem, should certainly have not frowned upon them remembering the destruction of the First Temple via a fast, as they too

---

[79] Jacob Milgrom, "Fasting and Fast Days," in <u>Encyclopaedia Judaica. MS Windows</u> <u>9x</u>. Brooklyn: Judaica Multimedia (Israel) Ltd, 1997.

were a part of the community of Israel. They may have not felt the compulsion to fast themselves, but if they were mature Believers they would have understood its importance. (Evangelical Christians today are certainly very sensitive to Jews and Messianic Jews who observe the Ninth of Av, even if they do not similarly fast.)

And so if the non-Jewish Believers in Rome would not look down on their fellow Jewish Believers for remembering some of these extra fast days—why would they criticize any Jewish Believers for not necessarily eating the meat available at some of their fellowship gatherings? What one chooses to eat, especially if food is being passed around at a table, or is laid out in a buffet, is entirely one's personal preference. If you are not going to judge a brother or sister for a major matter, why would you judge a brother or sister on a much smaller matter? If a non-Jewish Believer chooses to be unfair to a Jewish Believer over what is eaten at a fellowship meal, what could that communicate to the same Jewish Believer's other actions of faith? The Apostle Paul says,

"Let us therefore no longer pass judgment on one another, but resolve instead never to put a stumbling block or hindrance in the way of another" (Romans 14:13, NRSV).

Harsh judgment of other people, by putting unnecessary stumbling blocks in front of others, is somewhat tantamount to appropriating a job that only God Himself has. The Lord is the only One who can fairly judge a person, so the so-called "strong" judging the presumed "weak" in Rome needed to stop. What Paul described as dividing them were disputable opinions (Romans 14:1), to which each person will individually answer before Him.

Paul returns to the original issue, after making some points by talking about sacred days and not eating/fasting, and states what his opinion is on what is eaten in the fellowship meals:

"I know and am convinced in the Lord Yeshua that nothing is [common/*koinos*] in itself; but to him who thinks anything to be [common/*koinos*], to him it is [common/*koinos*]. For if because of food your brother is hurt, you are no longer walking according to love. Do not destroy with your food him for whom Messiah died. Therefore do not let what is for you a good thing be spoken of as evil; for the kingdom of God is not eating and drinking, but righteousness and peace and joy in the Holy Spirit" (Romans 14:14-17).

The Apostle Paul himself was not going to have a problem with what the Roman Believers might serve him when he comes to visit at their fellowship meals. If the Apostolic decree was being followed (Acts 15:20), even if the meat they served was from Roman sources—being "common"—such a status of being "common" is a disputable opinion. Yet Paul is very clear to emphasize to the Romans: those who eat such meat are not to use it as a tool to ruin other Believers. Yeshua the

Messiah died for the so-called "weak" Believers, who eat vegetarian, as much as He did everyone else, who might (arrogantly) consider themselves "strong." The Roman Believers needed to understand how "righteousness and peace and joy in the Holy Spirit" (Romans 14:17) are what are to make God's people different—far more than food. When this is the proper emphasis, than the people that God has made us to be can be realized:

"For he who in this *way* serves Messiah is acceptable to God and approved by men. So then we pursue the things which make for peace and the building up of one another" (Romans 14:18-19).

In closing up this vignette over the fellowship meals in Rome, Paul instructs,

"Do not tear down the work of God for the sake of food. All things indeed are clean, but they are evil for the man who eats and gives offense. It is good not to eat meat or to drink wine, or *to do anything* by which your brother stumbles" (Romans 14:20-21).

Paul affirms that whatever was being served at the fellowship meals among the Roman Believers was clean (*katharos*) by Biblical standards, but a person who uses the food with the intention of being an offense—because it might be "common" to some—commits evil. Rather than being an offense, it might be better to just not eat meat, drink wine, or make a huge issue out of something small, but large enough to cause another to stumble. Understanding the more conservative dietary opinions of some of the Jewish Believers in Rome, and the required sensitivity that the non-Jewish Believers should have had toward fast days, should enable these "strong" to restrict themselves in disputable matters should the situation require it. The issues are just not big enough to require any (more) significant divisions in the *ekklēsia*. In the words of James D.G. Dunn,

"Paul lays out the principle of self-restricted liberty in the most far-reaching terms: what applies to eating meat and drinking wine applies also to *anything* which causes a fellow believer to stumble and fall on his or her own pathway of discipleship."[80]

There were Jewish Believers in Rome, having returned after the expulsion of Claudius, who were going to have to get used to themselves being the minority. The non-Jewish Believers were not to complicate this due to disputable issues.

In the closing words of Romans 14, Paul finishes this instruction with a reminder on the individual's responsibility over the disputable matters of eating common meat, and sacred days of fasting:

"The faith which you have, have as your own conviction before God. Happy is he who does not condemn himself in what he approves.

---

[80] Dunn, *Romans 9-16*, 833.

But he who doubts is condemned if he eats, because *his eating is* not from faith; and whatever is not from faith is sin" (Romans 14:22-23).

When we decide to consider the background issues behind the whole of Romans 14, is it really about things like the Sabbath, appointed times, and even the kosher dietary laws now being issues of personal choice? Or, does it concern unnecessary divisions the Roman Believers were having at fellowship meals, and how if some Jewish Believers who fast on certain days were not to be criticized over their severity—why would anyone criticize some of them over the much more minor issue of not eating "common" meat? Too many of today's Christian readers of Romans 14 forget that a mixed grouping of Jewish and non-Jewish Believers, in First Century Rome, is being addressed. They also forget that the religious and social climate of that ancient time and setting is not the same as today.

The contemporary application can very much be seen in the spiritual and social dynamics of today's Messianic congregations. There are many Messianic Believers who are hyper-sensitive about the type of meat they eat. They will not eat clean meat unless it has a Rabbinical seal of approval on it, whereas at many Messianic congregations or homes more common meat from the local supermarket is served during fellowship times. This is the meat of Biblically clean animals, where the blood has been drained and soaked out with saltwater. But, the opinion of some is that it is too common, and that they will instead eat around. These are largely the same Messianic Believers who will be more prone to observe the many extra-Biblical fast days of Orthodox Jewish tradition, being convicted that it is helpful in their relationship with God.

The circumstances, that Romans 14 really does describe, are encountered in today's Messianic congregations all the time. How are we to handle them? Like Paul, I would eat at someone's table where "common," albeit Biblically clean meat, was being served, without any problem. As a teacher and spiritual mentor to many, just like Paul who served the Lord (cf. Romans 14:14a), I do not have the luxury of staying secluded to myself, in a protected environment where everything has to be certified "kosher"; I have to interact with the world at large. Yet I would be sensitive to the needs of those who are more cautious with what meat they eat. I would not at all look down upon certain Messianics who would not eat meat without a Rabbinical seal of approval, any more than I would look down upon them for not eating on various extra-Biblical fast days. I would pray that in their level of observance that they be blessed for their honoring of the Lord, and that I not unnecessarily offend them for their convictions.[81]

---

[81] For a further discussion, consult the author's article "How Do We Properly Keep Kosher?"

Many of today's evangelical Christians will be unable to consider this perspective of Romans 14. This is partially because resting on the Sabbath (much less observing the appointed times) has lost most of the significance it had for previous generations, including that of my parents—even if those previous generations of Christians kept a rigid "Sunday Sabbath." But most significantly, it is because the Christian Church of the Twenty-First Century is not the mixed body of Jewish and non-Jewish Believers as the *ekklēsia* of the First Century. Yet, Romans 14 does speak profoundly to the circumstances that many of today's Messianic congregations must work through—and so we must take important notice of Paul's word to the Romans, and not be unnecessarily divided over what are ultimately disputable matters. We must learn to uphold the Torah's instruction in Messiah (Romans 3:31), but similarly give grace to those who hold to different applications of it in terms of things like eating and fast days.[82]

In our efforts to keep *Shabbat*, the appointed times, and dietary laws—let us also not find ourselves unfairly judging our Christian brothers and sisters who do not keep them at present. Let us invite them to participate in them with us—as we are surely remembering these things as unto the Lord! Let us welcome them into our homes and congregations to experience His blessings!

What are we to do?

The interpretations that we have just considered of Galatians 4:9-11, Colossians 2:16-17, and Romans 14:5-6 will likely not be too popular in some parts of today's Christian community. These views do challenge some widely held opinions, but most especially they assert that many of today's evangelical Believers have not read these verses closely enough for what they meant to their original audiences. Are the appointed times really discounted in these verses as being important to Believers? Or are the misuse of the appointed times in false philosophy and pagan-influenced Judaism, and *halachic* matters regarding special fast days not explicitly required by the Torah, what compose Paul's original instruction?

When these verses are read a bit more carefully, for more than just sound bytes taken out of context, we are confronted with the reality that the Lord's appointed times were not annulled in the Apostolic Scriptures. They can easily be misused by various religious systems totally forgetting what their significance is as depicting God's plan of salvation history. And sadly, many people who keep the appointed times, and many people who do not keep the appointed times—often unfairly judge and criticize the other. Today's Messianic community

---

[82] For a further examination, consult the author's article "The Message of Romans."

needs to get beyond this, and needs to learn to become a voice of reason that can encourage all of God's people to take a hold of what the *moedim* represent for us who know Yeshua as Savior. These are not to be times of the year where we beat people over the head, or look down on others, but where we entreat the Lord to reveal Himself to us!

The Galatians were returning to practices not of God; the appointed times of the Torah *are* of God. The Colossians were being persuaded by an errant Gnosticized-Jewish philosophy against the Divinity of Yeshua that had hijacked Biblical practices as a part of its asceticism; they are told not to let the false teachers judge them because they see the Sabbath and appointed times differently, the Messiah being their substance. The Believers in Rome were told not to look down on others in the faith who chose to regard some days as sacred, choosing not to eat, because this is a matter of personal opinion; keeping the Sabbath and appointed times are commandments of God and are not human opinions.

The Biblical appointed times of the Torah in Leviticus 23 are things of the Lord and they are important for His people to observe—even more so as the Messiah's return draws near. They provide us every year with new insights as to how He will return, and the prophetic pattern that our Creator has set for the universe. They allow us significant opportunities to pause, and consider His plan for the ages. Most importantly they serve as important seasons that allow us to reflect on our spiritual standing before Him.

What are those of us who are Messianic to do about Christians who tell us that the Biblical holidays are no longer for us today? *They might not be willing to hear this exegesis of Galatians 4:9-11, Colossians 2:16-17, and Romans 14:5-6.* So, we must demonstrate by our praxis of faith—our faith lived out in the world—that celebrating the Lord's appointed times brings great blessings, spiritual insight, and above all enables us to express His love in unique ways.

Many Christians speak against the appointed times of God and do not know what they are speaking against. People such as these, sadly, often look down on us for obeying Biblical commandments that Messiah Yeshua likewise obeyed. In so doing, these people will reveal themselves to be, at the very least, immature in their spiritual walk. **They require our prayers;** they do not need mean-spirited criticism.

We need to take the higher road and not embroil ourselves in endless controversies with people such as these. We have to demonstrate to them that we are spiritually mature. Let God be the Judge of them if they do not share the convictions that we share. He as the Almighty Creator can certainly handle them better than we can. But let us also pray that these people will indeed repent and ask for forgiveness if they have wronged us. *And when that time comes, let us eagerly forgive them!* In the meantime, however, when criticized we need to be willing—through the power of the Holy Spirit—to forget it and move forward.

Many Christians do not judge Messianics at all for celebrating the Lord's appointed times, whether it be Messianic Jews honoring their heritage or non-Jews appreciating their Hebraic Roots. They are intrigued by them, and see some importance in them, but they just do not fully understand why we celebrate them and do not observe the holidays of Church tradition. In time, I believe that those loving evangelical Believers, who believe in fully following Scripture—not too dissimilar from my late father who brought the Passover into our Methodist Church—will be wooed by the Holy Spirit as we have. They will partake of the goodness of realizing the importance that the Lord's appointed times have for us, and will be convicted to keep them.

On the whole, we have much to look forward to, but helping others see the truth begins with us demonstrating a positive example, and not one of condemnation.

About the Author

John Kimball McKee is an integral part of Outreach Israel Ministries, and serves as the editor of Messianic Apologetics, an Internet website that specializes in a wide variety of Biblical topics. He has grown up in a family which has been in constant pursuit of God's truth, and has been exposed to things of the Lord since infancy. Since 1995 he came to the realization of the post-tribulational return of the Messiah for His own and the importance of the Jewish and Hebraic Roots of our faith. He is a graduate of the University of Oklahoma (Class of 2003) with a B.A. in political science, and holds an M.A. in Biblical Studies from Asbury Theological Seminary (Class of 2009). He is a 2009 recipient of the Zondervan Biblical Languages Award for Greek. John holds memberships in the Evangelical Theological Society, the Evangelical Philosophical Society, and Christians for Biblical Equality, and is a longtime supporter of the perspectives and views of the Creationist ministry of Reasons to Believe.

John is an apologist for the Creator God and in helping people understand their faith heritage in Ancient Israel and Second Temple Judaism. Much of his ministry in the past has been campus based to the multitudes in evangelical Christianity who are associated with a wide variety of Protestant denominations and persuasions. John has introduced college students to things that are Messianic such as the original Hebrew name of our Savior, Yeshua HaMashiach (Jesus the Messiah), a name that he has known since 1983.

John's testimony before his Christian friends at college challenged much of their previous thinking about the whole of the Holy Scriptures and the need to follow the commandments of the Most High. His college peers asked him many varied questions: Why do you not believe in the pre-trib rapture? What do you think of the *Left Behind* books? Why do you observe the seventh-day Sabbath? Why do you eat kosher? Why do you wear a beard? Why do you celebrate the feasts of Israel? Why will you use a *tallit* and wrap *tefillin*/phylacteries during private prayer? Why do you consult original Hebrew and Greek language texts of the Bible? Why don't you come to church with us on Sunday? This led John into Messianic apologetics and the defense of our faith. John strives to be one who is committed to a life of holiness and methodical Bible study, as a person who has a testimony of being born again and who sincerely desires to obey the Lord.

Since the 1990s, John's ministry has capitalized on the Internet's ability to reach people all over this planet. He has spoken with challenging, probing, and apologetic articles to a wide Messianic audience, and those Christians who are interested in Messianic beliefs. In the past decade (2005-2014), John has positioned himself as a well-needed, moderate and Centrist voice, in a Messianic movement which is trying to determine its purpose, relevance, and mission to modern society—a voice striving to sit above much of the posturing, maneuvering, and religious politics of the broad Messianic spectrum. Given his generational family background in evangelical Christian ministry, as well as in academics and the military, John carries a strong burden to assist in the development and maturation of our emerging Messianic theology and spirituality, so that we might truly know the mission of God. John has had the profound opportunity since 1997 to engage many in dialogue, so that they will consider the questions he postulates, as his only agenda is to be as Scripturally sound as possible. John believes in demonstrating a great deal of honor and respect to both his evangelical Christian, Wesleyan and Reformed heritage, as well as to the Jewish Synagogue, and together allowing the strengths and virtues of both Judaism and Christianity to be employed for the Lord's plan for the Messianic movement in the long term future.

J.K. McKee is author of numerous books, dealing with a wide range of topics that are important for today's Messianic Believers. He has also written many articles on theological issues, and is presently focusing his attention on Messianic commentaries of various books of the Bible.

J.K. McKee is the son of the late K. Kimball McKee (1951-1992) and Margaret Jeffries McKee Huey (1953-), and stepson of William Mark Huey (1951-), who married his mother in 1994, and is the executive director of Outreach Israel Ministries.

John has a very strong appreciation for those who have preceded him. His father, Kimball McKee, was a licensed lay minister in the Kentucky Conference of the United Methodist Church, and was a very strong evangelical Christian, most appreciable of the Jewish and Hebraic Roots of the faith. Among his many ministry pursuits, Kim brought the Passover *seder* to Christ United Methodist Church in Florence, KY, was a Sunday school teacher, and was extremely active in the Walk to Emmaus, leading the first men's walk in Madras, India in 1991. John is the grandson of the late William W. Jeffries (1914-1989), who served as a professor at the United States Naval Academy in Annapolis, MD from 1942-1989, notably as the museum director and founder of what is now the William W. Jeffries Memorial Archives in the Nimitz Library. John is the great-grandson of Bishop Marvin A. Franklin (1894-1972), who served as a minister and bishop of the Methodist Church, throughout his ministry serving churches in Georgia, Florida, Alabama, and Mississippi. Bishop Franklin was President of the Council of Bishops from 1959-1960. John is also the first cousin twice removed of the late Charles L. Allen (1913-2005), formerly the senior pastor of Grace Methodist Church of Atlanta, GA and First Methodist Church of Houston, TX, and author of numerous books, notably including *God's Psychiatry*. Among all of his forbearers, though, he considers his personality to be most derived from his late paternal grandfather, George Kenneth McKee (1903-1978), and his maternal grandmother, Mary Ruth Franklin Jeffries (1919-).

J.K. McKee is a native of the Northern Kentucky/Greater Cincinnati, OH area. He has also lived in Dallas, TX, Norman, OK, Kissimmee-St. Cloud, FL, and Roatán, Honduras, Central America. He presently resides in Dallas, TX, and is a member in good standing at Eitz Chaim Messianic Jewish Synagogue.

Messianic Apologetics is dedicated to producing high quality, doctrinally sound, challenging, and fair-minded publications and resources for Twenty-First Century Messianic people. Our broad faith community faces any number of issues requiring resolution—from newcomers to the Messianic movement and those who have been involved for many years. The books, studies, commentaries, and analyses provided by Messianic Apologetics intend to aid the legitimate needs of today's Messianic people, so they can have the answers they seek in their walk with the Messiah of Israel.

Titles are available for purchase at **amazon**.com.
www.outreachisrael.net or at

Hebraic Roots: An Introductory Study
is Messianic Apologetics' main, best-selling publication, that offers a good overview of the Messianic movement and Messianic lifestyle that can be used for individual or group study in twelve easy lessons

Introduction to Things Messianic
is an excellent companion to *Hebraic Roots*, which goes into substantially more detail into the emerging theology of the Messianic movement, specific areas of Torah observance, and aspects of faith such as salvation and eschatology

The Messianic Helper series, edited by Margaret McKee Huey, includes
a series of books with instructional information on how to have a Messianic home, including holiday celebration guides. After reading both *Hebraic Roots* and *Introduction to Things Messianic*, these are the publications you need to read!

Messianic Spring Holiday Helper
is a guide to assist you during the Spring holiday season, analyzing the importance of *Purim*, Passover and Unleavened Bread, *Shavuot*, and the non-Biblical holiday of Easter

Messianic Fall Holiday Helper
is a guide for the Fall holiday season of *Yom Teruah/Rosh HaShanah*, *Yom Kippur*, and *Sukkot*, along with reflective teachings and exhortations

Messianic Winter Holiday Helper
is a guide to help you during the Winter holiday season, addressing the significance of *Chanukah*, the period of the Maccabees, and the non-Biblical holiday of Christmas

Messianic Sabbath Helper

is a guide that will help you make the seventh-day Sabbath a delight, discussing how to keep *Shabbat*, common Jewish traditions associated with *Shabbat*, the history of the transition to Sunday that occurred in early Christianity, respecting those in the past who kept a "Sunday Sabbath," and an extensive analysis of Biblical passages from the Tanach (OT) and Apostolic Scriptures (NT) about the Sabbath, rest, and their relevance to modern-day Messiah followers

> also available is the five-chapter mini-book excerpt *Shabbat: Sabbath for Messianic Believers*, intended as a congregational handout

Messianic Kosher Helper

is a guide discussing various aspects of the kosher dietary laws, clean and unclean meats, common Jewish traditions associated with kashrut, common claims made that these are no longer important for Believers, and an extensive analysis of Biblical passages from the Tanach (OT) and Apostolic Scriptures (NT) about the Torah's dietary laws and their relevance

> also available is the five-chapter mini-book excerpt *Kashrut: Kosher for Messianic Believers*, intended as a congregational handout

Messianic Torah Helper

is a guide that weighs the different perspectives of the Pentateuch present in Jewish and Christian theology, considers the role of the Law for God's people, and how today's Messianics can fairly approach issues of *halachah* and tradition in their Torah observance

Messianic Apologetics editor **J.K. McKee** has written on Messianic theology and practice, including studies on Torah observance, the end-times, and commentaries that are helpful to those who have difficult questions to answer.

The New Testament Validates Torah
Does the New Testament Really Do Away With the Law?

is a resource examining a wide variety of Biblical passages, discussing whether or not the Torah of Moses is really abolished in the New Testament

Torah In the Balance, Volume I
The Validity of the Torah and Its Practical Life Applications

examines the principal areas of a Torah observant walk of faith for the newcomer, including one's spiritual motives

Torah In the Balance, Volume II
The Set-Apart Life in Action—The Outward Expressions of Faith

examines many of the finer areas of Torah observance, which has a diversity of interpretations and applications as witnessed in both mainstream Judaism and the wide Messianic community

Confronting Critical Issues
An Analysis of Subjects that Affects the Growth and Stability of the Emerging Messianic Movement

compiles a variety of articles and analyses that directly confront negative teachings and trends that have been witnessed in the broad Messianic community in the past decade

Messianic Apologetics has produced a variety of **Messianic commentaries** on various books of the Bible under the "for the Practical Messianic" byline. These can be used in an individual, small group, or congregational study.

general commentaries:
A Survey of the Tanach for the Practical Messianic
A Survey of the Apostolic Scriptures for the Practical Messianic

specific book commentaries:
Acts 15 for the Practical Messianic
Romans for the Practical Messianic
1 Corinthians for the Practical Messianic
2 Corinthians for the Practical Messianic
Galatians for the Practical Messianic
Ephesians for the Practical Messianic
Philippians for the Practical Messianic
Colossians and Philemon for the Practical Messianic
The Pastoral Epistles for the Practical Messianic
1&2 Thessalonians for the Practical Messianic
James for the Practical Messianic
Hebrews for the Practical Messianic

Follow Messianic Apologetics Online Via Social Medial

 www.messianicapologetics.net

 www.facebook.com/JKMMessianic

 www.twitter.com/JKMMessianic

 www.periscope.tv/JKMMessianic

 www.instagram.com/JKMMessianic

 www.youtube.com/MessianicApologetics

 www.pinterest.com/JKMMessianic

 plus.google.com/+MessianicApologetics

 podomatic.com/podcasts/messianicapologetics

45267283R00045

Made in the USA
San Bernardino, CA
04 February 2017